DRAMA
THEMES

Dedication

John Harvey and Leonard McHardy
– theatre friends, book friends, dear friends –

Acknowledgments

To:

- Those teachers across Canada who invited me into their classrooms
- The staff at *Theatrebooks*, for their support
- Jim Giles, Linda Lachine, John McLeod, Marion Vaclavik, and in memory, Lois Roy, for the friendship
- Debbie Nyman and Jeanie Nishimura, for the drama talk
- Bob Barton and Richard Courtney, for their words
- Warwick Dobson, Tony Goode and Jonothan Neelands, for the summer learning
- David Booth, for the seeds and the sowing

DRAMA THEMES

COMPLETELY REVISED

Larry Swartz

Pembroke Publishers Limited

©1995 Pembroke Publishers
538 Hood Road
Markham, Ontario, Canada L3R 3K9

Published in the United States of America by
Heinemann
A division of Reed Elsevier Inc.
361 Hanover Street, Portsmouth, NH 03801-3912
ISBN (U.S.) 0-435-08690-1

Canadian Cataloguing in Publication Data

Swartz, Larry
  Dramathemes

Rev. ed.
Includes bibliographical references.
ISBN 1-55138-052-8

1. Drama – Study and teaching (Elementary).
2. Drama in education.   3. Language arts (Elementary).
I. Title.

PN3171.S92 1995   372.6'6   C95-931396-6

A catalogue record for this book is available from
the British Library.
Published in the U.K. by
Drake Educational Associates
St. Fagan's Road, Fairwater, Cardiff CF5 3AE

Editor: Joanne Close
Design: John Zehethofer
Typesetting: Jay Tee Graphics Ltd.

This book was produced with the generous assistance of the
government of Ontario through the Ministry of Culture and
Communications.

Printed and bound in Canada by Webcom
9 8 7 6 5 4 3 2

Contents

An Overview

THEME	GAMES	DRAMATIC ACTIVITIES	SOURCE
Humor	Joining In	Choral Speaking	Rhyme
Mystery	Communication	Questioning/ Interviewing	Poem
Fantasy	Brainstorming	Creating Together	Picture Book
Animals	Physical Activity	Interaction	Fable
Relationships	Tableaux	Personal Storytelling	Picture Book
Folklore	Imagination	Storytelling	Folktale Fairy Tale
Community	Trust	Persuasion	Map
The Past	Concentration	Role	Novel
The Future	Negotiation	Improvisation	Poem
Multiculturalism	Co-operation	Interpretation	Script

About this Book

Dramathemes was written with the intention of giving teachers a traveling companion as they embark on drama journeys in their classroom. Since it was first published, many teachers across the country have thanked me for the practical ideas and structures that this guide offered them. To those teachers who were only beginning to use drama and sought strategies for introducing their students to the world of "Let's pretend" to those who were more experienced in using *Dramathemes* and shaped their own work around the structures provided, I thank you.

This completely revised second edition has been written to provide you with an updated version of games, activities, and sources surrounding the ten themes that framed the original book. The foundation of this resource remains the same since I have held the belief that literature can be the focus and springboard of drama explorations, and that themes provide a hook in the classroom for making connections to story and to fellow class members.

In this book, I have included a variety of genres such as picture book, poetry, fable, novel and script, not only as a means to suggest ideas for activities but also to engage the imagination and to enrich the creativity and thoughts of our students. The pages that follow describe some of my own experiences working with my grade three and grade five students in the Peel Board of Education, as well as with the hundreds of children I met in the past decade in my role as consultant.

The ten chapters of this book are based on popular thematic explorations in literature for young people:

- Humor
- Mystery
- Fantasy
- Animals
- Relationships
- Folklore
- Community
- The Past
- The Future
- Multiculturalism

It is my contention that these dramathemes can be used with all grade levels. Each particular group of youngsters is unique, and it is they, after all, who create the action. Your beliefs, experiences, training, and level of confidence will determine the starting points, the paths, and the ends you and your students will encounter on your journey. Select and modify ideas within the units to support your curriculum needs, your language program, and the interests and needs of your students.

To help you choose appropriate strategies, this edition of *Dramathemes* has been divided into:

Introduction
• an overview of the chapter's theme
• a listing of learning opportunities

Games
• activities, games, and exercises organized by skill focus and that introduce concepts explored in the theme

Dramatic Activities
• verbal and non-verbal activities to stimulate imagination, promote social growth, and develop improvisation skills

Extended Improvisation
• an exploration of a literature source
• a scheme outlining various phases to structure drama learning

Beyond the Drama
• extensions of the theme through writing, reading, art, and drama activities

Assessment
• observation guides, each with a focus area of language, social, and drama learning
• self-assessment profiles to help students reflect on learning

No book can serve as a definitive statement on practising drama. The titles that I have suggested in the Professional Reading section (p. 154) will provide you, I hope, with the same support they have given to me, and help you find further answers to your questions about teaching drama. That said, the answer to all of your questions won't be found on the pages of any book. The discovery and the learning for both you and your students will happen as you live through imagined experiences in your classroom.

1/Humor

TEACHER: What would you ask Miss Muffet if she came to the classroom?
STUDENT: Where did she go after she was frightened away?

. . . . .

Focus: Rhyme

There is no teacher's manual or curriculum guide to tell us where Miss Muffet went after she was frightened away, who she spoke to, or how she dealt with her problem. In this dramatheme, the strange situations in which rhyme characters find themselves invite the students into the world of humor where their imaginations can take charge.

Learning Opportunities
- To participate in games that develop group participation
- To practise the skills of interpretation by reading rhymes aloud chorally
- To familiarize students with the rhythms, patterns, and themes of a variety of rhymes
- To explore the stories within stories of playground and nursery rhymes
- To unravel the meanings of a short text by raising questions, hypothesizing, role playing, and improvising

Games: Focus on Joining In

Let's Shake on It

Students arrange themselves in a circle and count off in threes. Once all players have a number, they disperse throughout the room. On a signal, players wander about the room and shake hands with whomever they meet. If a player's number is "one," she or he shakes another player's hand once. If a player's number is "two," she or he shakes another player's hand twice. If a player's number is "three," she or he shakes another player's hand three times. The object of the game is to find players with the same number. When two players with different numbers meet and shake hands, one player will want to stop shaking while the other will want to continue. In this case, the players move on to find those players with the same number of shakes. When two players with the same number meet – they will know because of the number of handshakes given – they become teammates and move through the space together, looking for other players with the same number. The game continues until all players find their group.

Human Bingo

This is a suitable get-acquainted activity, or is appropriate to use when members of a class need to integrate with one another in a non-threatening way. The bingo sheet shown here can be used for this activity, or a class-made bingo sheet can be constructed. In this instance, members of the class offer a statement they wish to reveal about themselves. Each fact is recorded in one square. Students should be reminded to share only those facts that they consider public.

Each player has his or her own copy of the bingo sheet. The point of the game is to try to find a player who matches the information in a square. When players find someone who matches the information in a square, they ask him or her to sign it. The first player to fill a horizontal, vertical, or diagonal line calls out "Bingo." The game can continue by making the task more difficult, for example, the player must have filled in:

Has the same birthday as you	Has at least one initial the same as you	Wears glasses	Owns a cottage	Has been to Florida
Is not wearing running shoes	Has the same number of letters (first name)	Can say hello in three languages	Has two brothers	Is blonde
Has freckles	Has a cat	X	Likes liver	Has blue eyes
Is wearing shoes with laces	Prefers vanilla to chocolate	Has an allergy	Can play a musical instrument	Has a dog
Can do ten pushups	Is wearing something red	Likes doing crossword puzzles	Is smiling	Knows a nursery rhyme

- a specified line (e.g., the bottom line),
- two lines,
- four corners,
- an X (two diagonal lines),
- the entire sheet.

At the end of the activity, students share information that they've learned about their classmates.

Name Games

Forming Groups

In this game, students work in a variety of group situations as they seek others whose name shares a characteristic with their first name.

- Find others whose name starts with the same initial as their name, then line up alphabetically.
- Find others whose name shares at least two of the letters in their name.
- Find others whose name has the same number of vowels that their name contains.
- Find others whose name has the same number of letters that their name contains.
- Find others whose name has the same number of syllables that their name contains.

EXTENSION
- Students work with their last name.

Name Scrabble

Students unscramble letters in their first and last name to make as many words as possible. As an example, Alan Green makes the words *nag*, *lean*, and *seen* from his name. When they have exhausted all possibilities, students team up with a partner. Combining letters from both names, they make as many words as possible.

Thinking about Our Names

The following questions can be given to students to discuss, or to use as a questionnaire when interviewing one another.

- Do any words rhyme with your name?
- Without unscrambling any letters, what words can you find in your first name? in your last name?
- How many words can you make when you unscramble the letters of your first name?
- Who were you named after?
- Do you have a middle name?
- Do you have a nickname?
- Do you know your name in another language?

- What is the name of a pet that you know? How did the pet get its name?
- Do you like your name?
- What name would you choose for yourself?

Dramatic Activities: Focus on Choral Speaking

Choral dramatization invites students to read aloud such texts as rhymes and poems by assigning parts among group members. By working with peers to read aloud poems on a particular theme or topic or by a single poet, students take part in a creative activity that involves experimentation with voice, sound, gesture, and movement. Because of these variations, no two oral interpretations of a single poem are alike.

Choral dramatization enhances students' skills of reading aloud and presentation. More important, however, when students work in small groups to read aloud together, their problem-solving skills are likely to be enriched as they make decisions about the best way to present a poem.

Chanting Names

The following activities have students experiment with different ways of saying their names aloud.

Activity #1

Students practise saying their name in a variety of ways, for example, in a whisper, mysteriously, musically, as if being scolded, as if meeting a long lost friend, or as if being called by a robot.

Activity #2

In a circle, students take turns saying their name and performing an action. Other students call out the person's name as they mimic the action. For variation, students say their name in a way that differs from the others, for example, by shouting or whispering.

Activity #3

Using the total number of syllables in their first and last names, students clap a rhythm to accompany their name. As an extension, they create a movement/gesture to accompany each syllable of their name. Students then work in pairs to create a dance/movement that expresses both partners' names. This can be extended to groups of four.

Activity #4

Students think of an alliterative adjective to describe themselves (e.g., Sly Sally, Dynamic David, Amiable Amanda). On a signal, they walk around the room and introduce themselves (e.g., Hello, I'm Dynamic David) to as many people as they can in one minute. The activity is then repeated with the students acting in a manner that reflects their alliterative adjective. As an extension, students add an alliterative verb (e.g., Dynamic David digs), and mime the activity as they meet people.

Tongue Twisters

A fun way for students to practise read-aloud skills is to repeat tongue twisters. Students challenge others to see who can repeat most often one of the tongue twisters shown below and on the next page. They set a time limit for the challenge, for example, thirty seconds. Other strategies students may employ include using longer tongue twisters to be read alone, and dividing lines between partners or among group members.

- shining soldiers
- Ruth's red roof
- a proper copper coffeepot
- three free throws
- six seasick sheep sail slowly
- eight eager able eagles
- Nat's knapsack strap snapped

And these longer twisters...

> I saw Esau kissing Kate,
> And Kate saw I saw Esau,
> And Esau saw that I saw Kate,
> And Kate saw I saw Esau saw.

A tooter who tooted a flute
Tried to tutor two tutors to toot.
Said the two to the tutor,
"Is it harder to toot or
To tutor two tutors to toot?"

I thought a thought. But the thought I thought wasn't the thought
I thought I thought. If the thought I thought I thought had been
the thought I thought, I wouldn't have thought so much.

Clapping Rhymes

Many students are familiar with playground or nursery rhymes such as, "Miss Mary Mack Mack Mack," "Doctor Knickerbocker," "See, See My Playmate," and "A Sailor Went to Sea Sea Sea." They say these rhymes aloud with friends, often accompanying the rhymes with actions or clapping rhythms.

i) In this activity, students teach one another action rhymes, or add finger and hand actions to rhymes by clapping hands, snapping fingers, slapping knees, or clapping a rhythm with a partner. Students repeat the rhyme, increasing their speed each time or saying the rhyme in various ways, for example, from a whisper to a shout.

Peas porridge hot,
Pease porridge cold,
Pease porridge in the pot,
Nine days old.

My brother likes it hot,
My sister likes it cold,
My cat likes it in the pot.
Nine days old.

ii) There are more than ten body parts students can point to as they say this rhyme aloud.

Chester, have you heard about Harry?
He just came back from the army –
Everyone knows that he tickles his toes
Hip, hip, hurray for the army!

iii) Students perform accompanying actions as they chant each line aloud. They suggest other paired items or instructions that could be sung aloud.

Head and Shoulders Baby, One Two Three!
Head and Shoulders Baby, One Two Three!
Head and Shoulders Baby, One Two Three!
Head and Shoulders; Head and Shoulders; Head and Shoulders, Baby, One Two Three!

(patty-cake clap)
... Knees and Ankles Baby, One Two Three!
... Ears and Eyebrows Baby, One Two Three!
... Throw the Ball Baby, One Two Three!
... Milk the Cow Baby, One Two Three!
... etc.

Extended Improvisation: Using a Rhyme – "Little Miss Muffet"

The following drama structure encourages students to look inside and outside a piece of text. Because they are short, because there is opportunity to dig deeper into the narrative, because there is a possibility to uncover other stories within the story, because a problem or dilemma is suggested, rhymes are particularly effective for developing a drama unit.

A Scheme for Using Rhymes

Strategy	Function
Game	to set the context; to build interest
Choral Speaking	to experience the text
Discussing	to interpret and speculate
Questioning	to explore puzzles; to build commitment
Interviewing	to explore events; to build roles
Storytelling	to develop narrative
Meeting	to negotiate meaning; to problem solve
Reflecting	to investigate possibilities; to hypothesize
Extending	to explore the moment/the past/the future

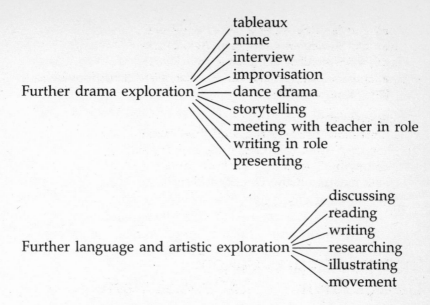

Further drama exploration
- tableaux
- mime
- interview
- improvisation
- dance drama
- storytelling
- meeting with teacher in role
- writing in role
- presenting

Further language and artistic exploration
- discussing
- reading
- writing
- researching
- illustrating
- movement

The following reflections outline my experiences using the familiar rhyme "Little Miss Muffet" with a primary class. Following the framework outlined on the previous page, I provided students with the opportunity to dig for stories and hidden truths. In addition to the rhyme, I used the picture book version by Ian Beck, in which the author presents the rhyme as a six-scene play and introduces such characters as a cat, a moon, and a crocodile. Students used these secondary characters to explore the rhyme from other points of view.

Game

Students worked with a partner. One student became the "clay", while the second student took on the role of sculptor. Sculptors were instructed to create a statue of a fairy tale hero or villain character with which they were familiar. Without speaking, they shaped the clay to create a pose of the character, using props if desired. Once sculptors finished their work, their partners tried to guess their identity. Students then switched roles.

Choral Speaking

As a group, we chanted the rhyme, "Little Miss Muffet." Students experimented by saying the rhyme in a variety of ways, including soft to loud, as a round, singing, clapping, and call and response. I gave each student a line from the rhyme. On a signal, they took turns reading their line. The activity was then repeated with each student saying the word as differently and dramatically as possible. Students concluded the activity by chanting their line, adding a movement, and then freezing.

Discussing

Students discussed the facts that they knew from reading the first four lines of the rhyme. They were also eager to offer their hypotheses of what happened to Miss Muffet, and many of their suggestions began with "maybe" (e.g., maybe the spider just wanted some food... maybe she was frightened by something else... maybe she had arachniphobia).

Questioning

I posed the following scenario to the students: "If Miss Muffet were to come to this room, what questions would you like to ask her?" Students informally discussed questions with their neighbors before sharing them in a whole-class discussion. I listed the following questions on chart paper:

- What is curds and whey?
- When did this happen?
- Do you always sit alone in the woods?
- Have you been on this tuffet before?
- Do you have any witnesses?
- What did the spider look like?
- What kind of spider was it?
- Did you talk to the spider?
- Who did you tell the story to?
- Where did Miss Muffet go after she was frightened away?

Interviewing

I asked the students to think about who, besides Miss Muffet and the spider, would be able to answer these questions. They suggested ten possible characters that could be used in the drama: a woodsman, Miss Muffet's mother, the spider's mother, Miss Muffet's teacher, her best friend, a doctor, a mouse, the moon, the tuffet, and Little Bo Peep. Some children volunteered to assume these roles. In turn, each character, in role, sat before the class to answer questions. I asked the students to think of an audience that would be interested in the characters' answers (e.g., detectives, Miss Muffet's family, newspaper reporters). To begin, students were invited to choose a role in which to ask questions when they met the character.

Further Interviews and Storytelling (In Role)

As characters told their version of the event, students began to build a narrative. Following the interviews they discussed what was known: Miss Muffet was alone in the woods, she likes curds and whey, she is an only child, she has this meal every Sunday afternoon, the spider was as big as a fist, the spider was more frightened than Miss Muffet. Students worked in small groups to interview the spider. Interviewers maintained their role and one student told the story from her point of view.

Meeting

A meeting was held where children revealed the stories that had recently been told. I assumed the role of Miss Muffet's teacher who was concerned that Miss Muffet would not return to school.

Reflecting (Presenting Images)

In groups, students created tableau images to tell the story. These images represented photographs that showed the guilt or innocence of the spider/of Miss Muffet.

- an image from her past that might explain why she was frightened,
- an image to show the image of Miss Muffet being frightened by the spider,
- an image to show where she went after being frightened,
- an image that would tell the story from the spider's point of view,
- an image to show what might happen the next time Miss Muffet sits on her tuffet.

Once prepared, students shared images which they presented chronologically. Audience members discussed what they saw in each scene and reflected on whether their questions were answered.

Reflecting (Meeting to Problem Solve)

As a group, students discussed why a spider might frighten someone. In role as relatives and friends of Miss Muffet, they discussed what advice they might give to the spider's mother (teacher in role) to stop her son from "bullying." As well, students suggested what might be done with the spider and what advice they might give Miss Muffet.

Extending (Writing)

Students reflected on their work by completing one of the following activities:

- adding a second verse to continue the story,
- giving advice to Miss Muffet or the spider via a letter,
- writing a story that explains why Miss Muffet is always frightened,
- writing a newspaper article covering the event,
- composing a diary entry Miss Muffet might have written,
- preparing a report about spiders to give to Miss Muffet so she is better prepared the next time she meets a spider.

Extending (Drama)

The Spider's Trial

- interview: detectives investigate witnesses to tell the "true" story,
- tableaux: photographs as evidence,
- improvise: scenes from the past to explain what happened (used as videotaped evidence),
- interrogation: the trial,
- decision making: the jury discusses guilt or innocence.

Hi i'm the man on the moon. I can see evrething. One day the cat and the fiddle saw Little Miss Muffet siting on her tafit. A spider camand scard her a way. He is in jail. The End.

Beyond the Drama

Mime Rhyme

Students work independently to create a mime of a familiar rhyme. Once they have planned their mime, they perform it for a partner who tries to guess the rhyme. Students may need to be reminded to slow their actions to help make their mime clearer.

Creating a Class Anthology

The class creates an illustrated anthology of recess or nursery rhymes with each student in the class illustrating one rhyme. Illustrations can be completed in a medium of the student's choice – cut paper, markers, crayons, tissue paper, and so on. Students determine whether illustrations will appear together or on separate pages.

Classifying Rhymes

Many anthologies present rhymes in sections or chapters according to a theme or characteristic. Using their class collection, students categorize their rhymes into sections. In small groups of four or five members, students take a copy of the poems and artwork and classify them in any way they wish, for example, by number of lines, by animal characters, or by gender. A problem-solving component can be introduced in the activity by limiting students to three categories for classification.

Further Reading

Students create classroom collections of other rhyme and pattern books under one of the following categories:

- alphabet books
- nursery rhyme collections
- counting books
- lullabies
- song books
- joke and riddle books
- rhymed stories

Working in groups to gather books for one category, students create an annotated bibliography. Group members choose their favorite book from each category and share it with the rest of the class.

Assessment: Focus on Choral Speaking

Name: _____ Date: _____

Does the student:	Always	Sometimes	Never
1. Use voice appropriately to convey mood and intent?	☐	☐	☐
2. Recognize his or her role in the ensemble?	☐	☐	☐
3. Contribute ideas to the choral presentation?	☐	☐	☐
4. Support the contributions of others?	☐	☐	☐
5. Have an appropriate sense of audience?	☐	☐	☐
6. Follow directions and accept advice?	☐	☐	☐
7. Experiment with pitch, pause, and pace to make the reading more effective?	☐	☐	☐
8. Investigate possibilities of using voice, sound, and movement?	☐	☐	☐
9. Understand the importance of revising and rehearsing?	☐	☐	☐
10. Seem committed to the task?	☐	☐	☐

Comments:

_____

_____

_____

_____

_____

_____

_____

_____

2/Mystery

"We all need to be the kind of teacher who stops to ask, 'Why are we doing what we're doing?'"

Shelley Harwayne, *Lasting Impressions* (1992, p. 192)

. . . . .

Focus: Poem

Mystery stories and poems let us journey into places and problems that are not part of our real lives. Solving the mystery is like following an old treasure map — you have to add all the clues and details to come up with a solution, correct or otherwise. In this dramatheme, the students become drama detectives caught in a mystery web woven with question marks and imagined stories.

Learning Opportunities
- To practise communication skills through oral word games
- To develop skills of questioning, both in and out of role
- To conduct interviews by taking on a role
- To describe and explain ideas in small and large groups
- To negotiate meaning with others by responding to a poem

Games: Focus on Communication

Word Association

This popular word game invites players to voice spontaneous thoughts that arise in response to words spoken by another player. Players should be encouraged to associate freely and needn't explain their word associations. The game begins by having one player say a word, for example, "book," "water," or "tree." The second player responds to that word by saying the first word that comes to his or her mind. The first player then responds to that word. Play continues until one or both players decide to end the game.

EXTENSIONS

- The game is played in groups of four.
- Players clap a rhythm between words.
- Players respond with words that have no association to the last word spoken (e.g., water, bench).
- Players write their answers. Later, they shape the words into a poem or script. Pairs can exchange their work to read aloud.

Sixes

Students sit in a large circle. One player is chosen to sit in the centre with his or her eyes closed. On a given signal, an object (e.g., ball, ruler, pen) is passed around the circle from neighbor to neighbor. At any point in time, the player in the centre claps his or her hands. The player who has the object is now "It." The player in the centre calls out a letter of the alphabet – "It" must name six objects that begin with that letter within the time it takes for the object to be passed to him or her again. (If the circle is small, the object can be passed around two times.) If "It" is successful, the game continues with the object being passed until the player in the centre claps his or her hands, whereupon the process begins again. If "It" cannot name six objects beginning with that letter, she or he replaces the player in the centre.

- Players specify criteria, for example, each word must have two syllables, or fit a category (e.g., cities, animals, foods). The rule of each word beginning with the same initial can be maintained, depending on the age of the group.

I Packed My Bag #1

Students sit in a circle. The first player says, "I packed my bag and in it I put a toothbrush." The second player says, "I packed my bag and in it I put a toothbrush and a violin." The third player packs a toothbrush, a violin and something new, for example, a banana. Each player repeats in order all that has gone before and adds a new object. To make the game more challenging players name objects in alphabetical order, objects that begin with the same letter, objects that have two syllables, or objects that are accompanied by an adjective.

I Packed My Bag #2

The rules are the same as the traditional "I Packed My Bag" game, but instead of saying "toothbrush," for example, players act out an activity that involves that noun. As examples, "toothbrush" may become an action of brushing one's teeth; "violin," the playing of the instrument. Each player repeats in order all that has gone before and adds a new mime.

Dramatic Activities: Focus on Questioning and Interviewing

Witness

Students work in pairs or small groups. One person is chosen to be the storyteller/witness; other players are to be the lawyers. The lawyers are free to interrupt the storyteller at any time and ask him or her details that will add to the story being told.

WITNESS: One day last summer...
LAWYER: What day was it?
WITNESS: It was a Thursday.

LAWYER: What was the temperature that day?
WITNESS: It was very hot.

EXTENSION
- Students take turns so that everyone has the chance to role play both the storyteller and a lawyer. They may change the group size and the number of people telling the story.

Gathering Evidence

For this activity, students work in groups of four. (1) Each group is given a large envelope. Members fill the envelope with eight to twelve objects from their pockets, knapsacks, or desks. Students are asked to imagine that these objects all belong to the same person, and that they have been gathered as evidence against him or her by the police. As a group, students use the objects to build a story around this character. (2) After each group has worked out the background of their character, they pass their envelope to another group. Two of the members move with the objects and two remain behind so that new groups of four are formed. (3) On a signal, the police (the two original partners) reveal their evidence to the private investigators (the two new partners). The private investigators try to determine the story behind the evidence. The police should be prepared to answer questions, but do not have to tell investigators everything they know. (4) Students return to their original group and develop or revise their story based on the investigators' questions and explanations.

EXTENSIONS
- Students conduct a whole-class improvisation where each detective group uses its evidence to present a case. Students, as investigators, try to connect the stories.
- Students continue the investigation by calling witnesses to testify.

What's the Question?

Like the television show, "Jeopardy," this activity invites students to think of questions that can accompany statements. As an example, if the statement is "school," questions might be: "Where do you go every morning?" "Where do you learn things?" and "What do you call a group of fish?" Students can provide questions for the following statements:

1. in the attic
2. in the newspaper
3. Bermuda
4. beside the cottage
5. I was frightened!
6. green
7. it's too hard
8. my uncle
9. money
10. No way!

Students, individually, in pairs or in small groups, write at least three questions that correspond to each statement. (If there is time, they provide questions for all statements.) Once they have completed their lists, they join other students to compare questions.

EXTENSIONS

- With a partner, students choose three questions they think are most dramatic. They improvise a conversation between two characters, using one of the questions. Students decide beforehand who might be speaking and why they might be having this conversation.
- As an alternate activity, students work with a partner to conduct a conversation in which both participants can only ask questions. The challenge is to maintain the conversation as long as possible without the use of a statement.

News Report

Each student clips a picture of one person from a magazine or newspaper. The pictures should feature people who interest the students in some way, perhaps because of their expression or pose, or because of the setting of the photographs. To make the activity more valid, students should choose pictures of unknown people, rather than celebrities. Students become newspaper reporters. Their job is to interview the people in the pictures. They think of five or six questions they would like to ask of the person whose picture they have chosen. Once students have prepared their questions, they choose three questions that they believe will yield the most interesting information. Students work with a partner to conduct an interview. One student role plays the part of a person in a photograph; the second, the part of a newspaper reporter. When finished, they switch roles. After the improvisation, students work independently to write their newspaper article. If necessary, they replay their roles in order to generate more information for their articles.

Students are told that their two characters are both going to appear in a newspaper's front page article. What do these characters have in common? Why might their story be on the front page of a newspaper? What headline will they use for their article? Together, each pair of students plans, as reporters, a story that they think might appear in a featured news report. With their partner, students create a frozen tableau that represents the front page photograph of the newspaper article. As a final activity, students conduct a news conference where each pair of students shares their news story. Pairs present their stories in role as reporters, or as characters from the pictures. In the latter instance, the rest of the class assumes the role of newspaper reporters conducting a group interview.

EXTENSIONS

- Partners write the newspaper article as it might appear on the front page of the newspaper. They include a headline and picture that might appear on the front page.
- Partners write their newspaper article as an interview. They use some or all of the questions they prepared for their interview.
- Partners share their article with another pair of students. Groups of four brainstorm what the four characters have in common.

Note: Students could use actual newspaper or magazine articles. Once they have read an article, they prepare questions to ask of one or more of the featured characters.

Extended Improvisation: Using a Poem – ''The Key of the Kingdom''

This dramatheme focuses on exploration of a poem through a variety of activities, including: choral speaking, drawing, storytelling, questioning, and drama. The following pages outline my experiences with this dramatheme while working with a split grade three/four class.

The Key of the Kingdom

This is the Key of the Kingdom:
In that Kingdom there is a city;
In that city is a town;
In that town there is a street;
In that street there winds a lane;
In that lane there is a yard;
In that yard there is a house;
In that house there waits a room;
In that room an empty bed;
And on that bed a basket –
A basket of sweet flowers:
    Of flowers, of flowers;
    A basket of sweet flowers.

Flowers in a basket;
Basket on the bed;
Bed in the chamber;
Chamber in the house;
House in the weedy yard;
Yard in the winding lane;
Lane in the broad street;
Street in the high town;
Town in the city;
City in the kingdom –
This is the Key of the Kingdom,
    Of the Kingdom this is the Key.

Anonymous

Choral Speaking

Students practised reading the poem aloud in a variety of ways:

- each student in the class was assigned one line of the poem. (Depending on the number of students in the class, some lines could be read in pairs, others by the whole group.)
- I read each line of the poem, omitting the last word for students to fill in:

TEACHER: This is the Key of the...
CLASS: Kingdom.

TEACHER: In that kingdom, there is a...
CLASS: city.

- the class was divided into two groups. Lines were divided so that each group was responsible for reading these words aloud:

GROUP A: This is the key
GROUP B: ...of the kingdom.
GROUP A: In that kingdom
GROUP B: ...there is a city.

Once students were familiar with choral speaking techniques, they were assigned to one of six groups: three groups recited parts assigned to "A," three groups recited parts assigned to "B." Groups reciting Part A worked to prepare a choral presentation of the first verse; groups reciting Part B, a choral presentation of the second verse. Each group decided how to present the poem aloud, with some lines read solo and some lines repeated. Students were encouraged to experiment with voice and gesture. When all groups had prepared their choral dramatization, they shared it with others. All groups gave advice to others for improving the presentation.

Illustrating the Poem

Students worked in pairs for this activity. Each pair was assigned a single line from the first verse of the poem. Using a large sheet of chart paper and markers, they created an illustration to accompany the line. This was a suitable activity to have students develop the story behind the poem. As they created images, they provided clues about the key, the kingdom, the city, the town, the street, and so on. Once completed, illustrations were arranged in sequential order. Each pair of students introduced their illustration and explained details they had included. Class members examined each illustration and determined what they had learned from this data. Students developed a story about the kingdom by making connections and determining patterns in the illustrations.

Storytelling #1

Students were arranged in a circle. As the key was passed around the circle, each student revealed one statement about the key.

Statements focused on its discovery, its importance, and its mystery. Students began their statements with the words, "This is the key that...." As students played this storytelling game, they passed an actual key from one person to the next. Once each student had contributed a sentence, the class discussed patterns and connections that had emerged as a result of the students' contributions.

Storytelling #2

This activity was most effective with groups comprising six to eight students. On a signal, Person #1 in each group began to tell a story about the key. She or he continued the story until a signal was given to change. Person #2 continued the story until the signal was repeated. The activity progressed until the students were asked to stop. Since there was a relatively short time between changes, some students made two contributions to their group's story.

EXTENSION

• Each student found a partner from another group. One partner told his or her group's story while the partner asked questions. When finished, the partners reversed roles.

Raising Questions

Working in small groups, students prepared a list of questions related to items mentioned in the poem – the key, the kingdom, the city, the house, the room, its contents, and so on. To help focus the students, I assigned each group two or three lines of the poem. Students brainstormed a number of questions about the lines they had been assigned. Groups recorded these questions in lists. When all groups had finished this task, each group worked with a partner group to determine common questions. All groups gathered to discuss questions that appeared most frequently and those that were considered most vital by individual groups. As students worked through subsequent drama activities, they found some answers to their questions and also developed new questions.

Creating the Room

Students were divided into two groups. One group worked to prepare the room mentioned in the poem. Members used furniture, equipment, clothing, pictures, and posters that were available in the classroom. Through the creation of this room, students made a space that represented the place where the drama occurred. As they defined the space, they offered others an opportunity to read symbols as well as help to build a context for the drama. During this time, the second group of students retired to a quiet part of the room where they drew up a list of questions they expected would be answered by inspecting the room arrangement. Once the set was complete, students who had devised the questions offered interpretations about the inhabitant(s) who lived in the room. As well, they offered hypotheses about what happened to the person or people who had lived in the room.

Forum Theatre

In forum theatre, a situation is enacted by any number of players while the rest of the group observes the action. Observers can step in and take over roles, or add suggestions to make the scene more authentic. Forum theatre allows students to explore a variety of attitudes to an event as they work through it in drama. In forum theatre, the audience can stop the action from time to time in order to make suggestions about characters' dialogue and behaviors. Scenes are repeated so that suggestions can be implemented and analyzed.

Students brainstormed a list of possible characters. Some students volunteered to assume the role of one of these characters. Using the set as a focus of exploration, the scene was brought to life by introducing a character who might have been in the room at one time. The audience controlled the scene's action by offering suggestions about where the character should sit, stand, or move. What actions would she or he do? What behaviors would she or he demonstrate? The class then introduced a second character into the scene. Students playing these characters began to improvise a conversation.

The Key to the Kingdom: The Play

The class was divided into five groups, and each group was invited to create a scene that would tell some part of the key's story. Since groups worked independently, each group interpreted its instructions in any way it wished. Once each group had prepared its scene, they shared it with the rest of the class. Students discussed how the scenes connected. From the information presented in the scenes, they determined which of their questions concerning the key and the kingdom had been answered.

Scene 1: The Need for a Key

Who ordered the key to be made? Why was a key needed? Who controlled the use of the key?

Scene 2: The Creation of the Key

How was it created? discovered? invented? What materials were used to make the key? What designs appeared on the key?

Scene 3: The Flowers, The Room, The Key

What is the significance of the flowers, the basket, the room, and the house in the story of the key?

Scene 4: A Problem with the Key

Was the key broken? stolen? lost? Who could help solve the problem? What would happen if there was no key?

Scene 5: The Rescue of the Key

Who knows the true story of the key? How can the key be protected? How important is the key to the future of the kingdom?

Beyond the Drama

Writing Poetry

Students create their own poem patterned on the form of "The Key of the Kingdom." By changing nouns in the poem, they write a new mystery poem. Instead of focusing on a key, poems can focus on a box, a map, a bottle, or a treasure.

Map

Using the information from the poem, students work as a class to create a map of the kingdom. They contribute to the design of the map by adding buildings, monuments, features, homes, and businesses that might have formed part of the kingdom. This activity helps students develop a context for the drama, similar to the illustration activity described on p. 102.

Story Writing

Students are asked to imagine that a historical document is being made in order to record important events in this community. Students use information from their drama to write a history of the key, the kingdom, the empty bed, or the basket of sweet flowers. By compiling stories, they create a book entitled "The History of...."

Inventing a Game

Students invent a game based on the poem and their improvisations. While some students may want to develop a physical game that is suitable for outdoor or gymnasium play, other students may want to develop a board game. Students form groups based on the type of game they want to develop. In both instances, however, they must use a key as a prop. Once members of each group decide on the rules of the game – number of players, equipment, penalties, and so on – they explain the game to others in the class. As well, they write out instructions so others can play the game independently.

Assessment:
Focus on Communication Skills

Name: _____ Date: _____

Does the student:	Always	Sometimes	Never
1. Reveal thoughts willingly?	☐	☐	☐
2. Explain and describe ideas clearly?	☐	☐	☐
3. Take turns during discussions?	☐	☐	☐
4. Accept and build on the ideas of others?	☐	☐	☐
5. Make positive suggestions to complete tasks and build the drama?	☐	☐	☐
6. Raise questions?	☐	☐	☐
7. Conduct interviews effectively?	☐	☐	☐
8. Communicate thoughts in role?	☐	☐	☐

Comments:

_____

_____

_____

_____

_____

_____

_____

_____

_____

_____

_____

3/Fantasy

"Our inner drama is what makes us human. We think 'as if' – we imagine. Then, as a result, we act 'as if.' Imagining lets us consider possibility, and it is this which is uniquely human."

Richard Courtney, *The Dramatic Curriculum* (1980, p. 1)

. . . . .

Focus: Picture Book

The drama journey takes us to places both real and imagined. Through drama we can explore life around the corner, in other kingdoms, or on other planets. In this dramatheme, the private world of imagination can be shared with others as the students travel to the moon without leaving the classroom.

Learning Opportunities
- To use imagination and creativity to complete tasks involving art, music, and drama
- To brainstorm and examine several possibilities to a problem
- To develop social skills by working in a variety of group situations to solve problems
- To look at an issue from different points of view by assuming different roles
- To share and learn facts about the moon

Games: Focus on Brainstorming

Creativity Inc.

Students work in pairs or in small groups to complete this creative thinking activity. They are asked to imagine that they work for a company called Creativity Inc. Their job at the company is to develop lists of ideas to help others think creatively. The following items are some problems that must be solved by the employees of Creativity Inc. Depending on the number of students working together, they pick one to five problems (more if they wish) to solve:

1. List things that are soft.
2. How many ways can you use a rope?
3. How would you entertain a crying baby?
4. Name foods that have double letters.
5. What jobs will there be in the future that do not exist today?
6. Name things that have holes.
7. How many ways can you win something?
8. How many words can you make from the word "dinosaur"?
9. What are some ways to recycle a plastic cup?
10. Invent new ice cream flavors.
11. Describe a world without numbers.
12. Describe a world without books.

Students compare their completed lists to assess their own level of creativity as well as that of others.

What's the Use?

Students are challenged to name as many ways items on the next page can be utilized. As an example, a button could be used as an earring, the eye of a teddy bear, a surfboard for a tadpole, a placemat for wet spoons, and so on. Students are reminded that in brainstorming all responses are to be accepted. As well, they are told that they must be prepared to explain their answers. To ready the students for brainstorming, they might work together as a whole group to record ways a plastic cup may be used. Each pair or small group of students could then be assigned the same item, or could be assigned a different item from the list.

- a tree branch
- an umbrella
- a bead
- a chair
- a sock
- a broom pole
- a candle
- a suitcase
- a roll of masking tape
- an empty bottle

EXTENSION

- Students use an object such as a pencil, a roll of masking tape, a ruler, or a chair. Sitting in a circle of five or six, they are told that they are going to use the item to perform a mime activity. The magical item can be transformed into anything they'd like. As an example, the first person uses it as a baseball bat while the second person uses it as a tightrope. After each person has performed an activity that demonstrates what the item has become, she or he passes it to the person on the right. If that person can't think of an activity, she or he can say "pass." The game continues until the students run out of ideas.

Packing for the Moon

Students are asked to imagine that they have been selected to go to the moon. Each person can carry one knapsack of personal items – all supplies, foods, medicines, and other necessities will be available on the moon. An experienced astronaut will guide them to ensure their safety. To begin, students work individually to prepare their list of what they will take in their knapsack. They have ten minutes in which to prepare their list before they form small groups. In their groups, they share their lists. Students are then told that there has been a change of plan. Only one knapsack per group will be allowed on the spaceship. This means that each student can take only two items. Students review their list and decide on the two items they will take.

EXTENSION

- Students discover that they must bring with them all items needed to survive on the moon. In groups, students work together to prepare their packing list. As well, they must decide if personal items will be allowed.

Dramatic Activities:
Focus on Creating Together

Paired Drawings

This activity can be used to demonstrate non-verbal communication and to examine interaction and co-operation. Students work in pairs. Each pair is given a large sheet of paper and one crayon. They are asked to hold the crayon together so that both draw at the same time. On a signal, students are asked to create a picture, but they are not allowed to speak. Both students hold the crayon simultaneously and proceed to draw until they have finished their picture to each partner's satisfaction. After the activity, students discuss how they felt about this activity. How did the two partners communicate? Did they co-operate? Was there a leader? Are they satisfied with the picture?

Note: To help students, some music might be played as they draw their pictures, or students might create a drawing in response to a poem or a story.

EXTENSION

• The activity could be repeated by allowing the partners to speak, having students find a new partner and not speaking, or assigning a specific picture to be drawn.

Soundtracking

> Soundtracking gives students the opportunity to create an environment using their voices, the sounds of hands or feet and, if available, musical instruments. The sounds that students create, which can be realistic or stylized, tell a story, create a mood, or convey a sense of place. At times, soundtracking can be paired with dialogue to explain a scene, or to allow actors to give voice to their thoughts.

The following situations give students practice in soundtracking:

- walking through a haunted house,
- landing on the moon,
- witnessing an alien invasion on Earth,
- being caught in a storm,
- illustrating war and peace.

In small groups, students tell the story of one scene through sound. When members of each group have finished their sound improvisation, they create a scene for the rest of the class. Audience members sit in a circle or in a private space and experience the improvisation with their eyes closed.

Moon Creations

Students are asked to imagine that they are astronauts who have just landed on the moon. They form small groups of three or four astronauts. Their task is to create a space station from a package of materials included on one of the astronaut's space ships. The package (a large envelope) contains items such as newspapers, tin foil, cardboard, paper plates, tubes, straw, and string. Each group is given one package of materials. Before students begin building, they are asked to comply with one condition – they can communicate only on a non-verbal basis. On a signal, students begin to build their space station. It is not necessary to impose a time limit on this activity. Students may work until they feel satisfied with their station, or they have used all their materials. The process usually takes between fifteen and twenty minutes. Completed space stations are displayed and viewed by other groups. The activity ends with a whole-class discussion that gives students a chance to air their feelings on working silently as part of a group.

EXTENSIONS

Students may talk during any of these activities.

- As an alternative, students create creatures that they might discover on the moon, monuments that could be left on the moon as souvenirs from earth, and space vehicles.
- As a group, students create a four- to six-line rhyming poem that accompanies their creation. Poems, which can be written

on cards, inform other astronauts of the space station and what they may expect to find there.

- Groups prepare a choral reading of their poems. Members decide how each line should be read, how parts will be divided, and what movements or positions will be used to present the poem.

Extended Improvisation: Using a Picture Book – *Architect of the Moon*

The following lines open *Architect of the Moon* by Tim Wynne-Jones:

> A message arrived from outer space
> A message from the moon.
>
> *Help! I'm falling apart. Yours, the Moon.*

This story introduction serves as a focus for drama exploration by having the students raise questions, invent roles for people who receive the message, write in role as those who sent the message, or report their discoveries from the moon. The drama can be slowed by having the class make preparations for a visit to the moon. As the drama builds, students might create an actual "visit" to the moon. Though a fantasy theme, the drama structure offers students opportunities to reveal and learn information about space through a fictional context.

The structure also allows for flexibility of exploring place, time, role, and conflict. This dramatheme outlines alternatives to develop an effective structure that deals with a fantasy situation. The following scheme serves to outline the options that a class might experience as moon explorers.

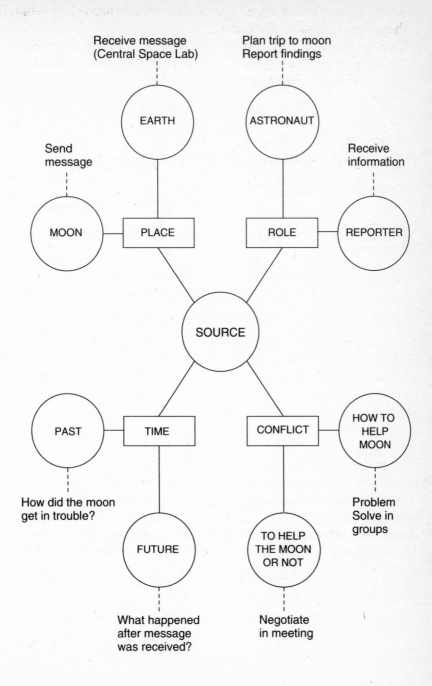

Receive message
(Central Space Lab)

Plan trip to moon
Report findings

EARTH

ASTRONAUT

Send
message

Receive
information

MOON

PLACE

ROLE

REPORTER

SOURCE

PAST

TIME

CONFLICT

HOW TO
HELP
MOON

How did the moon
get in trouble?

Problem
Solve in
groups

FUTURE

TO HELP
THE MOON
OR NOT

What happened
after message
was received?

Negotiate
in meeting

Alternative contexts for exploring this dramatheme

This reflection describes my experiences with two primary classes using *Architect of the Moon* (with thanks to Charlotte Haines and Harriet Melin's classes in Saskatoon and Rosthern, Saskatchewan respectively).

Session One: Exploring a Message from the Moon

Phase One: Discussing the Moon

Students discussed stories about the moon. Together we listed facts that they knew about the moon.

Phase Two: Setting the Context by Writing a Message

I showed the first page of the story *Architect of the Moon* and read the opening lines – ''A message arrived from outer space / A message from the moon.'' Students then speculated on what the message from the moon might have been, and suggested ideas for the contents of this message. I wrote the message, which turned out to be a rhyme, on a piece of chart paper.

> I need your help,
> I am losing my light,
> Before I disappear,
> Please make things right!

Students experimented with different ways of reading the message aloud.

Phase Three: Speculating and Raising Questions

Students made further speculations about why the moon might be losing its light. A brief discussion was held about how people on earth might help the moon. Students raised questions that they would ask the moon if they had the chance to speak to it personally.

• How long have you had this problem?
• Have you had any damages/injuries?
• Is anybody angry with you?
• Where do you get your light?

Phase Four: Meeting in Role

To help students develop roles, I asked them to answer these three questions:

- Who might have received the message?
- Where was the message received?
- How was the message received?

An emergency meeting was held at Central Space Lab where students, in role, discussed how they received the message. They invented their roles (e.g., doctors, scientists, astronomers, children), and revealed their invented stories to answer the three questions.

- I was in my space lab and a message came over the computer.
- I was just about to shut off the television when a message appeared on the screen.
- The moon came into my bedroom and whispered the message in my ear.
- When I woke up this morning I saw the message written on my mirror.
- When I took a bath I saw the message written on my tummy.
- The message was scratched into the bark of a tree in our backyard.

Students then wrote the message they received from the moon.

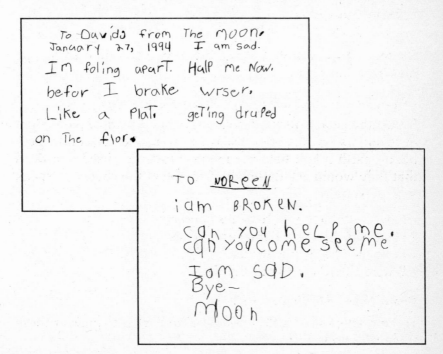

At the conclusion of the meeting, students came out of role to discuss what they learned about the moon messages. They had the opportunity to clarify their roles and, if they wished, change them for future drama exploration.

Phase Five: Writing in Role

Students were given the chance to send a message to the moon advising it of how they could help. For this message, students were encouraged to ask questions, give advice, or suggest how they might help the moon. When finished, I collected their messages.

Session Two: Preparing to Visit the Moon

Phase Six: Interviewing the Moon

I gave each student a message and asked them to read their message in role as the moon. In role as commander of the Central Space Lab, I then held a meeting with the students who formed a circle and assumed the role of the moon. Students answered questions I posed as the commander and had the chance to learn more about the moon's predicament.

Phase Seven: Preparing for the Moon

Students returned to their roles of the previous day to discuss preparations for helping the moon. They decided that they would like to help the moon and felt they could do as this as astronauts. First, they would have to prepare for their mission. They formed four groups; each group discussed one of the following topics:

• what equipment would be needed,
• what questions would be answered during the mission,
• the training an astronaut would need to visit the moon,
• what the space vehicle would look like and how it would work.

A representative from each group presented a report, and explained what group members viewed as necessary preparations for their trip to the moon.

Phase Eight: Designing Sets

Activities such as designing sets help students build commitment to the drama. In this theme, they formed two groups. The first group used found equipment in the classroom to build a space vehicle that would be suitable for traveling to the moon. The second group created an environment (e.g., buildings, landscape, people, equipment) that astronauts would see on their arrival at the moon.

Phase Nine: Soundtrack

Once completed, each group had a chance to inspect the other's set before creating an accompanying soundtrack (for more on soundtracks, see pg. 42). To build their soundtracks, students could use their voice, hands, dialogue, or music. Group members created a soundtrack for the environment they created. The first group shared their soundtrack by having members of the second group close their eyes while they listened. The other group then repeated the process.

Session Three: Solving the Problem

Phase Ten: Making Plans to Help the Moon

Students decided that the cause of the moon's fading light was pollution. Working in role as scientists, they prepared plans that would help the moon return to its normal state. Each of the plans was drawn on a large sheet of paper. Students met once again in the Central Space Lab where a panel discussion was held about dealing with the moon. Representatives from each group gave a report and questions were raised by fellow scientists.

Phase Eleven: Creating Images from the Moon

Students created tableau images to tell the moon's story. To set the context, I explained that astronauts who had visited the moon took photographs to record their visit. I asked students to form small groups. In their groups, they created two images: an image that showed how the moon lost its light, and an image that showed the moon in the future, after it had been repaired.

Beyond the Drama

Reading and Retelling Stories about the Moon

Students form literature circles with each group reading a picture book about the moon (see Recommended Books, p. 149). Once groups are familiar with their stories, members use the jigsaw method to form new groups that have at least one member from the original group. These students retell the story that their group read and answer questions about the selection. If this is the first time students have worked in this group situation, they might retell the story to a partner.

Visual Report: Life on the Moon

Students choose one of the following items that they, as astronauts, might have discovered on their visit to the moon:

- an animal
- a school
- a playground
- a plant
- a vehicle
- a machine
- a teacher
- a game or sport

Students speculate what their item might look like and create a drawing to bring back to earth. To make their drawing more official, students add labels, descriptions, or explanations about the item they have investigated. They then meet in role as astronauts and share their discoveries by presenting an oral report. Alternatively, sketches could be displayed in a space museum, or assembled into a book entitled "Life on the Moon."

Reporting from the Moon

Students investigate information about the moon using, if they like, facts gathered during the dramatheme. They present their information in one of the following ways:

- as a report written in role of an astronaut who visited the moon (might appear in the form of an astronaut's log or notebook),
- as a fictitious interview with the moon who recounts his life and experiences,

- as a quiz or test, that is, students prepare true or false, multiple choice, or fill-in-the-blank questions to test a peer's knowledge about the moon,
- as a tape-recorded message that might be sent by a moon explorer back to earth.

All about the Moon

Students work with a partner or in small groups of three. Each group is assigned one of the following topics for brainstorming:

- words with "oo"/words that rhyme with "moon"/words that have "moon" as a root,
- titles of rhymes and songs about the moon,
- books and films about the moon,
- sayings or expressions about the moon/myths about the moon,
- things I know about the moon,
- things I wonder about the moon.

Each topic is printed on a large piece of chart paper. Students record their responses. On a signal, they move to another sheet and add items that they think belong on that sheet. The activity is repeated several times. Students discuss the sheets as a large group, volunteering any additional information they can add.

Inventing Stories

Students use the following questions as a stimulus for inventing stories about the moon. They work in small groups to create a collaborate narrative.

- What if the moon fell apart?
- What if the moon was captured?
- What if the moon disappeared?
- What would happen if the moon fell to earth?
- What if the moon was a different color?
- How was the moon invented/discovered?

EXTENSIONS

- Students tell the story in role as a character who visited the moon, lived on the moon, or was a friend of the moon.
- Students prepare a written version of their oral moon story to share with others in the school.

Student Self-Assessment:
Focus on Group Participation

Name: _____ Date: _____

1. What did you enjoy about the activity?

   _____

2. Were there moments when you worked independently?

   _____

3. Did someone else's idea help you?

   _____

4. Did you feel frustrated at any point in the activity?

   _____

5. Was there a leader in your group?

   _____

6. How did you co-operate with other group members?

   _____

7. What did you do if you didn't like someone else's idea?

   _____

8. How could this group have worked more efficiently?

   _____

9. What might you do to improve your finished product?

   _____

10. What else would you like to say about working in groups?

   _____

   _____

4/Animals

"Nurturing, sustaining, and encouraging the kind of inquiry that helps children to understand more deeply must surely be central to the work with stories."

Bob Barton, "Learning Them by Heart" in *The Drama Theatre Teacher* (Winter 1993, p. 13)

. . . . .

Focus: Fable

This dramatheme invites the students into the kingdom of four-legged, two-legged, and no-legged creatures. By stepping into the paws of our animal friends, students are given the opportunity to explore the shared world of humans and animals.

Learning Opportunities
- To develop physical growth through games and movement activities
- To interpret and understand the concept of proverbs
- To explore the themes and morals of fables through retelling, storytelling, and improvising
- To practise revision and rehearsal in order to present work to an audience using Story Theatre and Readers Theatre
- To explore the world that human and animals share by investigating literature with anthropomorphic characters

Games: Focus on Physical Activity

Tortoise and Hare

The group sits or stands in a circle. Students are told that one ball represents the tortoise, and a second ball the hare. The ball representing the tortoise is to be passed around the circle in a clockwise direction from player to player. The ball representing the hare can be thrown around the circle in any direction. The object of this game is for the hare to catch the tortoise. This occurs when one player is passed the tortoise ball and is thrown the hare ball at the same time. The game is then repeated.

EXTENSION

• To make the game more complicated, a third ball is introduced as a second hare. Eventually a fourth ball, representing a second tortoise, is introduced.

Safari

Students sit in a circle to form a "jungle." They number off from one to five and give themselves the following identities: one – cheetah; two – elephant; three – ape; four – rhino; five – zebra. An animal is called out, for example, zebra. This is a signal for all zebras to run around the outside of the circle and get back "home" as quickly as possible. The last person to reach home becomes the caller for the next round. Once students are familiar with the game, the caller says the names of two animals. When the word "safari" is called, all players must run around the circle and return home.

EXTENSION

• Animal words are substituted with those corresponding to a special theme or story.

Building a Zoo

This activity has students working spontaneously in a variety of group situations. Students must work with different people in each situation, and should only work with the same class member once. The students' task in this activity is to create a zoo by using their bodies to represent various animals. On a signal, students work:

- alone to make a snake,
- with a partner to make a swan,
- in groups of three to make a tarantula,
- in groups of four to make a giraffe,
- in groups of five to make an elephant,
- in groups of six to invent a new animal for the zoo,
- to repeat any of the above.

EXTENSION
- Students make furniture for a house, for example, a lamp, plant, kitchen sink, stereo, and portrait.

Letters and Numbers

This game requires students to interpret instructions imaginatively at the same time that they use their body for flexible movement. There are several variations that can be used in this game:

- a letter is called out – students attempt to make their body look like the letter (they can do this on their own or with a partner),
- students make the letter look a certain way according to instructions, for example, make the letter as wide as possible, make the letter lowercase and as small as possible,
- in groups of three or four, students answer questions by using their bodies (e.g., spell "dog," show the total age of your group).

What's In a Name?

This activity has students working imaginatively to interpret instructions and develop movement skills. To begin, students write their names in the air. They are then instructed to use only part of their body (e.g., their left ear, their right shoulder) to write their name. The activity can be varied through requests for large and small movements, the use of imaginary equipment (e.g., a feather, a hose), and name variations (e.g., writing their last name or the name of a friend, writing their initials).

- Instead of their names, students spell different words.
- The activity is done as a mirror activity. Students copy a partner's movements.
- Students send messages to a partner by writing it in a mutually shared space.

Move Along!

This activity is best done in a large space, such as a gym. Students should be encouraged to interpret the instructions in their own way, and not be swayed from their interpretations by their friends' movements. Students are asked to move from one side of the room to the other:

- with one foot and one hand on the floor,
- with no feet touching the floor,
- with their head on the floor,
- backwards, and in slow motion,
- in a swirling motion,
- like a kangaroo,
- like a spider,
- like a monster,
- in as few moves as possible,
- moving silently,
- attached to another person,
- as if they were in a blender,
- as if their feet were tied together,
- as if the floor was made of glue,
- as if the floor was made of hot sand.

EXTENSION

- Students work in groups of four or five. They determine how they would move across the room if they were all tied together, and if the group were tangled.

Dramatic Activities: Focus on Interaction

Proverbs

If students aren't familiar with proverbs, a class discussion outlining their intent will be helpful. Students work with the following proverbs, or with others with which they are already familiar:

1. Look before you leap.
2. Birds of a feather flock together.
3. Beauty is in the eye of the beholder.
4. Never put all your eggs in one basket.
5. The early bird catches the worm.
6. A bird in the hand is worth two in the bush.
7. A fool and his money are soon parted.
8. You scratch my back and I'll scratch yours.
9. Every cloud has a silver lining.
10. Blood is thicker than water.
11. A rolling stone gathers no moss.
12. A stitch in time saves nine.
13. Forewarned is forearmed.
14. Necessity is the mother of invention.
15. All that glitters is not gold.

Students complete the following activities to increase their familiarity with proverbs.

Proverb Charades

Students work in small teams. One player is shown a proverb. Within a set time, that player must mime the proverb she or he has been shown. Teammates try to guess the proverb.

Proverb Pictionary

Students work in small teams. One player is shown a proverb. Using a marker and a piece of paper, that player draws the proverb. Like "Charades," teammates try to guess the proverb. This game could be played as a relay with teams competing against one another. Each player should have a chance to illustrate a proverb.

Fractured Proverbs

Players write out a well-known proverb, leaving no space between words, for example, arollingstonegathersnomoss. Next, players break up the letters at random intervals, for example, ar oll ingst oneg ath er snomoss. Players exchange papers to determine who can most quickly decipher the proverb correctly. Once players have practised the game, they repeat the activity using other less-known proverbs.

EXTENSION

• In groups, students invent a gibberish language by reading the proverbs aloud a number of times.

Proverb Stories

Students form small groups. Working with a proverb of their choice, group members discuss the meaning behind the proverb. Together, they invent a story that shows the intent of the proverb. Students should be encouraged to move beyond the literal meaning of the lines, that is, they do not have to show "two birds in a bush." Students tell their story to other groups.

Dramatic Presentations of Proverbs

Each group chooses one proverb. Group members discuss the meaning behind the words and prepare an improvisation that demonstrates its moral. There are several ways students can present their improvisation: each student assumes a role, students use narration only, or they present an improvisation comprising narration and mime tableaux. Groups share their improvisations. Audience members discuss the moral or lesson portrayed in each improvisation and try to identify the proverb.

Extended Improvisation: Using Fables

Fables

"Years and years ago, someone thought up a clever way of telling other people the truth without being rude. You

58

made up a story, often about animals. It might seem funny, but it was serious underneath."

Mark Cohen, *The Puffin Book of Fabulous Fables* (1989, p. 9)

Fables are short stories that usually feature animal characters and end with a moral or lesson. Because they are short, fables are suitable texts for exploring Readers Theatre, Story Theatre, puppet presentations, storytelling, and improvisation.

The following strategies outline various ways that fables can be experienced. The variety of activities were shared with my grade three class over a five-day period. Students can work with a single fable, or gather a variety of fables from various collections to share with others. Although fables are the focus for this unit, the strategies are useful with other folktales, particularly those that are not lengthy.

Though a fable is a suitable resource for having students explore interpretation, they also come to understand morals or messages of fables through improvisation and creating analogous situations.

The Wolf and the Dog

The poor wolf was cold and hungry: the weather was bad and he had not had a decent meal for many days. Then, one dark night, he found a farm and there in the middle of the yard was a hen house. He was licking his lips and thinking out his plan when he was disturbed by a fierce bark. Turning, he came face to face with a bulldog. The wolf studied the dog and noticed how well he looked.

"Why do you look so warm and well fed?" asked the jealous wolf.

"I am the master's friend," replied the dog. "I help protect his family and farm. In return he houses and feeds me."

The wolf was full of envy, until he noticed the chains. "What are these?" he queried.

"They are just my chains," informed the dog. "They ensure that I do not wander off."

The wolf was shocked. "You can keep your warmth and food," he said. "I would rather be hungry and free, than in chains like a slave."

Moral: *It is better to be free and poor than rich and enslaved.*

The Wolf and the Crane

One day a wolf was eating his dinner when a bone lodged in his throat. The poor wolf coughed and coughed but it was no use; the bone was stuck and he lay there gasping for breath.

A crane wandered by and the wolf pleaded for help, but the bird ignored his cries and carried on walking.

"If you help me," gasped the wolf, "I'll make sure you are well repaid."

The crane stopped. "You will reward me?" he questioned.

"Yes, yes," groaned the wolf. "Please help!"

The wolf opened his mouth, the crane removed the bone, and waited for his reward.

"There is no further reward, you silly bird," laughed the wolf. "Was it not enough to put your head in a wolf's mouth and not have it snapped off?"

"But I was so kind," complained the crane. "I have saved your life."

"You were not kind," snapped the wolf. "You only saved me for a reward. "

Moral: *No favor is a kindness, if done for a reward.*

Day One

Students can use the morals of various fables to develop stories and situations that demonstrate a lesson being taught. Morals included in this section accompany the selections in *Aesop's Fables*, illustrated by Safaya Slater. One of the following morals can be chosen – the class creates an improvisation that demonstrates the lesson.

Morals can also be assigned to pairs or small groups of students for discussion. Groups then prepare an improvisation that demonstrates the lesson and present it to others. The audience guesses the moral or lesson presented in each improvisation.

• Be happy with what you've got.
• One good deed deserves another.
• Wise people learn from their neighbor's mistakes.
• You will often be judged by the company you keep.
• You can't please everyone all the time.
• Sometimes it is better to bend with the wind than stand against it.
• The fruits of hard work are the best treasure of all.
• Don't make excuses for what you know to be laziness.
• Unity brings strength; division brings only weakness.
• Selfishness brings its own punishment.

As students plan their performance, they should consider questions such as the following:

- Which characters are needed to tell the story?
- Will they use animal characters?
- Where will the story take place?
- In what time period will this story take place?
- What lines of dialogue will be said?
- How can narrators enhance the storytelling?
- Where will characters stand or sit, and what actions will they do?

Day Two

Readers Theatre

In Readers Theatre, a script is developed from material that was not initially written for performance. The techniques of Readers Theatre allow participants to dramatize narration and dialogue using selections such as fables. Readers Theatre does not require students to memorize lines, but before they read a piece aloud they should have the opportunity to think about and discuss the characters they will interpret.

Choral speaking techniques can be very successful in Readers Theatre. Timing and pacing can be as expressive as the sound of the readers' voices. Readers Theatre can also be visual; for example, the group can create stage pictures or tableaux to enhance the script. Since listeners concentrate on the spoken word, gesture and movement should be used sparingly. There may be moments, however, when a significant movement by one or more characters heightens the dramatic impact.

In Readers Theatre, a decision needs to be made about how to present narration as well as dialogue. For instance, each performer might read lines of the narrator that describe his or her character's thoughts and actions, or the narrator's lines might be read in chorus. The intent of Readers Theatre is to present a piece of literature intact, although all the words need not be presented. If all words are included, some experimentation should be done with phrases like "he asked" and "said the lion" that often appear at the beginning, middle, or end of a line.

Some Readers Theatre presentations can be made more dramatic through the use of masks or simple costuming, as long as they do not interfere with vocal clarity and projection.

Story Theatre

Story Theatre differs from Readers Theatre in that all the action and movement in a story is played out. It also gives students the opportunity to dramatize materials other than scripts. The basic technique is that in addition to lines of dialogue, students or a separate group of performers play out the action implied or described by the lines.

Before interpreting a selection in Story Theatre, the group assigns roles. When there are more roles than performers, some students will play more than one role. When there are more performers than roles, more than one student will play each role, or portray an inanimate object necessary for the story.

Story Theatre makes use of simple settings and properties. A coat, a scarf, or a hat may be all that is required in addition to ordinary clothing. Songs, sound effects, tableaux, and movement can enhance a presentation. Story Theatre is also a suitable format for older students to work with younger students.

Day Three

Scripting Fables

Because fables are relatively short, they are a suitable resource for having students prepare scripts. Working with a partner or small groups, students practise reading the fable aloud in order to become familiar with both spoken and narrated parts. It might be necessary to demonstrate how script dialogue differs from prose dialogue.

Now, bears are very fond of fish, so Bear asked Fox if she would share her catch.

"No," said Fox. "I need them all for myself."

"How can I catch my own then?" Bear asked.

"Oh it's easy," said Fox. All you have to do is cut a hole in the ice..."

NARRATOR: Bears are very fond of fish and so he asked Fox if she would share her catch.

FOX: No. I need them all for myself.

BEAR: How can I catch my own then?

FOX: Oh it's easy. All you have to do is cut a hole in the ice...

To begin, students determine which characters will be needed for the presentation of their fable or folktale. They then decide if a narrator will be used, and if yes, how many narrators will be needed. Alternatively, students may decide to assign a character's role(s) to read lines of narration.

As students prepare the script, they should feel comfortable about eliminating, changing, or adding lines of dialogue to make their script read more smoothly. Students might also make suggestions for the way lines should be read, and the way characters should sit, stand, or move. They may also make suggestions on gestures and expressions to be included. One way to determine whether students have been successful at script writing is to have groups exchange and read aloud one another's scripts. Fables can then be collected into a class script for others to perform.

Puppetry

Students might use fables as a source for creating a puppet presentation. Using the strategies suggested in Story Theatre, students have the puppets assume various roles of characters and narrators. A puppet presentation is also an alternate way to have students present a script.

Day Four

Storytelling

Students use the plot of fables to practise storytelling skills as they retell the events of a story. They can tell stories in a class circle, in a small group, or with a partner.

STORYTELLING #1: RETELLING THE STORY

On a signal, one person begins to tell the story. When the signal is given again, the person beside him or her continues the story. Students should be encouraged to add as much detail as they wish.

STORYTELLING #2: RETELLING IN ROLE

As an extension to the first activity, students retell the story in role as one of the fable or folktale's characters. If working in groups, students decide which character might tell the story. Each storyteller then contributes by speaking in role as that character.

Students retell the story by conducting an interview between someone who wants to find out about the story (e.g., a relative of a character, a visitor to the community, the media) and one of the characters in the story. Those who are telling the story in role can change or add details as they are questioned during the interview.

Beyond the Drama

Day Five

1. Students write a fictitious journal entry from the point of view of one of the characters, explaining the lesson that she or he learned and how it was learned.
2. Students create an illustration to accompany the fable.
3. Students use a fable's moral or lesson to write a new fable based on the same moral.
4. Students change the setting and/or the characters to create a new version of a fable they have read. The fable might take place in a particular time or place. These new versions can be dramatized or written.
5. Two characters from different fables meet to discuss their experiences. Students work in role to interview one another, compare adventures, and explain lessons that were learned.
6. Students use movement to present the fable as a dance drama. They employ appropriate music to accompany their presentation.
7. Students retell the story of a fable as a comic strip.
8. Students imagine that many years have passed. They assume the role of a character who learned a lesson in a fable. What stories will this character tell his or her grandchildren about the lesson learned years ago?
9. Students research habits of one of the animals that they read about in a fable. They list all that they know about the animal before they prepare a list of unanswered questions.
10. Students discuss fables: How is a fable different from other stories? What is appealing about fables? Why are animals used rather than people? What is a moral? What is your favorite fable?

Assessment:
Focus on Physical Activity

Name: _____ Date: _____

Does the student:	Always	Sometimes	Never
1. Enjoy playing physical games and participating in movement activities?	☐	☐	☐
2. Work well with partners, in small groups, and with the whole class?	☐	☐	☐
3. Trust and support others?	☐	☐	☐
4. Express ideas using various parts of the body?	☐	☐	☐
5. Appear energetic?	☐	☐	☐
6. Comply with instructions?	☐	☐	☐

Comments:

_____

_____

_____

_____

_____

_____

_____

_____

_____

_____

_____

_____

_____

5/Relationships

"The stories we tell and listen to shape who we are. They give body to our own experience and take us beyond the confines of everyday life – into the past, the future, the might be."

Susan Engel, *The Stories Children Tell*, (1995, p. 57)

. . . . .

Focus: Picture Book

When the picture book character Wilfred Gordon McDonald Partridge seeks an answer to the question, "What's a memory?" he inspires readers to reflect on the stories of their lives. In this dramatheme, students will have the opportunity to explore the events and relationships that shape the self. By creating and inspecting the identities and relationships of fictional characters, students can illuminate memories that light the corners of the mind.

Learning Opportunities
- To communicate ideas non-verbally through tableaux
- To reflect upon and share personal stories
- To develop and understand a character's identity by inventing events, stories, characters, props, and images
- To use a picture book to create a fictitious past and explore memories
- To write in a variety of genres using the context of drama as a stimulus

Games: Focus on Tableaux

Memory Tableaux

This activity develops students' understanding of tableaux. Though this might be a familiar strategy for most students, their work on creating a photo album or still images of a life allows them to focus on various aspects of presenting. In the first part of the activity, students work in groups of three to create a memory album of a family's photographs. If they have had experience in creating tableaux, they can be instructed to create their pictures without talking. The following captions, which will accompany the pictures, are called out:

1. Baby's First Step
2. The Little League Game
3. A Shopping Trip
4. Oops!
5. Congratulations!

Students prepare tableaux that represent memories of their own lives, memories of a story character, or real photographs. Using one group's tableaux, these criteria can be demonstrated to the class:

Multi-levels: Are students arranged in high, medium, and low positions?

Balance: Is the arrangement balanced? Is spacing between figures reasonable?

Focus: What is the scene's focus of attention? Where will the viewer's eye rest?

Captions from the first part of the activity are called out. Students should be encouraged to revise their tableaux using the criteria of levels, focus, and balance. As well, they can be reminded of the effectiveness of appropriate facial expression and gesture.

EXTENSIONS

- Students create a new photo for the memory album that brings to mind an exciting, embarrassing, sad, or troublesome family moment. Once students are satisfied with their tableaux, they create two additional photos — taken moments before and after the scene — that might appear in the album.

- Before sharing their scenes, students should be satisfied that they have followed the criteria for creating tableaux and can move comfortably from scene to scene (transitions). As groups present their memories, audience members suggest captions that they think might accompany the memory.
- Students depict a memory scene through movement. Imagining that the memory was captured on videotape with no sound, students depict the scene through mime.

Family Reunion

This game has students working in flexible groups. Sets of four to six cards, depending on the number of students in the class, are printed with family names; for example, Father Jones, Mother Jones, Sister Jones, and Brother Jones; Father Stein, Mother Stein, Sister Stein, Brother Stein, Cousin Stein, and Grandmother Stein. Each student is given a card. Students wander the room and exchange cards with anyone they meet. On a signal, students first look at their cards and then find their families. Once all members are present, families retire to one corner of the room and create a tableau representing a photo in the family album. The game is replayed several times.

EXTENSIONS

- After playing the game several times, students remain with one family to create three pictures for the family album. Captions to accompany the photos can be suggested; for example, our family vacation, Happy Birthday, at the amusement park, a surprise, and an embarrassing moment.
- Groups are formed by having all fathers, mothers, sisters, brothers, cousins, and grandmothers meet for a group picture.
- Students combine with another group to create a photo with eight or twelve family members. They decide who will be in the family photo. Each student should be encouraged to take another role than the one she or he played in the original photograph.
- The following activity is somewhat more sophisticated, but could develop into a dramatic exploration of family relationships. Students are told that not all family pictures are displayed in a photo album. They are asked to imagine that a family has hidden one picture, perhaps because it reveals a sad time, a

secret, or a disturbing relationship. Students, in their family groups, discuss the story behind the picture and create a frozen tableau to depict the moment. Students bring the photos to life by revealing their inner thoughts.

Dramatic Activities: Focus on Personal Storytelling

Stories from My Past

Students pick one of the following topics or questions on which to base the retelling of a personal, significant story. They provide as much detail as possible, and answer audience members' questions concerning their story.

1. What was your best vacation?
2. Which teacher do you best remember?
3. What was your most memorable birthday party?
4. Have you ever been in danger?
5. When have you been afraid?
6. What special toy(s) have been part of your life?
7. What special accomplishment have you achieved?
8. What book do you remember from your childhood?
9. Have you ever repaired anything?
10. Have you ever been admitted to a hospital?
11. Have you ever had stitches?
12. Tell about a time that you had to move.
13. Describe a time when you were surprised.
14. Describe a time when you "learned your lesson."
15. Has a close family member or friend died?

Alternate storytelling methods include:

• Students are given a time limit to tell their story.
• Students are assigned a topic. They work with a partner or small group to develop their story.
• After listening to a story, students might work with a new partner or group and tell the story that they were told.
• Students work as a whole group to tell stories relating to the topics and questions. On a signal, one student begins to tell his or her story. On another signal, she or he stops and another

student picks up the story. Each person has a chance to contribute to the collective storytelling.

- Students take turns telling stories that come to mind when they hear the following words. Their stories can be about themselves, about someone they know or have heard about, or perhaps books they've read and movies they've seen. What story comes to mind when they hear the word...

lost	campfire	embarrassed
lonely	seashore	storm
accident	shopping	museum

Sharing Personal Memories

For this activity, students work with several partners for brief periods of time. Students form two circles (an inner and outer circle). Facing one another, they begin a conversation by telling something that they did last weekend. After a short period, students are given a signal to change. Members of the inner circle stay where they are while members of the outer circle move one step to the right. Conversations may or may not be suggested (e.g., an enjoyable movie, an embarrassing moment, a favorite meal). Some conversations may be brief; some will last a few moments.

EXTENSIONS

- When students arrive back to their original partner, each partner exchanges stories she or he heard.
- Students further practise their storytelling skills by retelling, in first-person voice, a story they heard from a classmate.

What's a Memory?

A new dictionary is about to be published, but "memory" has yet to be defined. Students, as dictionary editors, have been called upon for their input. On a piece of paper, students write what they think is a definition of memory. They then work with a partner to compare definitions and, if necessary, combine ideas to create a single definition. In small groups, students prepare a definition of "memory." To make the activity more challenging, their definition must be exactly twenty words long. The class conducts a meeting of dictionary authors. As a group, they decide on entries for memory.

EXTENSION

- Students are told that the new dictionary is strictly visual and that all definitions must be represented without words. Students create an image or design that represents memory.

Note: This activity is useful for introducing a theme or concept. I have used it successfully for students to define the words "drama," "friendship," "poetry," and "peace."

Extended Improvisation: Using a Picture Book – *Wilfred Gordon McDonald Partridge*

"When we write memoir, we must discover not only the moments of our lives, but the meanings in those moments."

Lucy McCormick Calkins, *Living Between the Lines* (1991, p. 177)

The activities in this section reflect my experiences with a curriculum unit I completed with my grade three and grade five classes after reading Lucy McCormick Calkins book, *Living Between the Lines*. In it, Calkins quotes Virginia Woolf: "A memoir is not what happens, but the person to whom things happen" (p. 166). Narrative helps students to inspect chronological details of an event; memoir allows students to explore the significance of an event. Like writing, drama allows students to re-create worlds at the same time as it celebrates, represents, and reflects on the stuff of our lives.

The picture book *Wilfred Gordon McDonald Partridge* by Mem Fox is an ideal resource for exploring the theme of memoirs. In this story, a small boy tries to discover the meaning of "memory" so he can restore the memories of an elderly friend, Miss Nancy Alison Delacourt Cooper. (Throughout the unit, students referred to the character as Miss Nancy.) This resource provided a meaningful context for integrating language and art as students recreated memories of a fictitious character and reflected on their own memories.

Picture books on a memoir theme are suitable for drama exploration, particularly since the pretend experience allows participants to manipulate time. Students inspect the moment of a memoir, as well as the time preceding and following it. In addition, memoirs allow students to create roles as they explore relationships of characters in a text and a drama.

Several picture books listed in the Recommended Books section (p. 149) are suitable for drama exploration. In particular, those books that are illustrated as photographs (e.g., *Reunion*, *Grandma's Bill*, *The Red Ball*) offer a starting point for recreating images. Students then unravel the feelings, story, and meaning behind each image.

In this dramatheme, I have provided one model for planning lessons from a story. These webs might be useful when planning lessons using a text as a resource.

Ten strategies to frame the learning

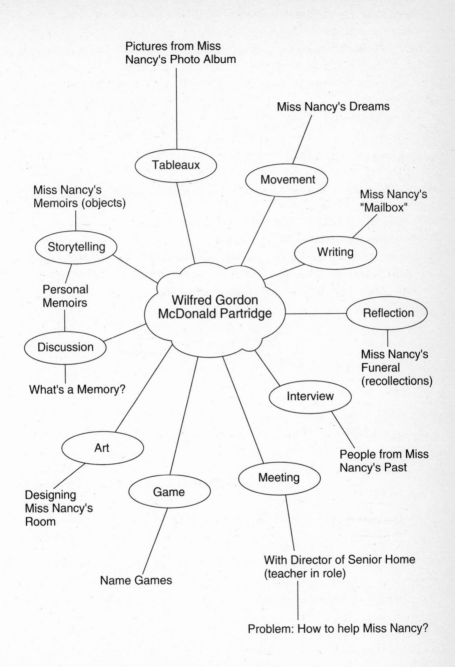

Pictures from Miss Nancy's Photo Album

Miss Nancy's Dreams

Tableaux

Movement

Miss Nancy's Memoirs (objects)

Miss Nancy's "Mailbox"

Storytelling

Writing

Personal Memoirs

Wilfred Gordon McDonald Partridge

Reflection

Discussion

Miss Nancy's Funeral (recollections)

What's a Memory?

Interview

Art

People from Miss Nancy's Past

Designing Miss Nancy's Room

Game

Meeting

Name Games

With Director of Senior Home (teacher in role)

Problem: How to help Miss Nancy?

Contexts for experiencing the strategies

Wilfred Gordon McDonald Partridge

1. Game

CONTEXT

Wilfred and Miss Nancy both have four names. Students had the opportunity to play name games and tell stories about their own names (see Unit One, p. 14, for additional name games).

ACTIVITY

The game of "Atom" requires students to group spontaneously according to instructions. In my class, students grouped according to these qualifiers:

- people who had the same number of letters in their first name,
- people who had the same number of syllables in their first name and their last name,
- people who shared the same two vowels in their first name,
- lined up alphabetically, with five per group,
- people whose first or last name started with the same initial,
- people who were born in the same month – students then looked for commonalities in names.

EXTENSION

In pairs, students used all the letters from their first names to spell and list as many words as possible.

2. Discussion

CONTEXT

In the story, Wilfred seeks the answer to the question, "What's a 'memory'?"

ACTIVITY

Students discussed their notion of memory. They touched on kinds of memories, triggers for memories, the importance of memory, and what happens when a person loses his or her memory. Some students took the opportunity to share some personal memories – sad, happy, exciting, funny, and embarrassing situations they remembered.

"What's a Memory?" (see pg. 70) may be a useful activity to introduce at this time.

3. Storytelling

CONTEXT

In the story, Miss Nancy is reminded of her past by objects that Wilfred presents to her.

ACTIVITY

Students worked in groups to prepare stories that would accompany each of the objects that Wilfred Gordon presents to Miss Nancy. Once students had prepared the stories, they created an improvisation that showed the importance of these objects in a scene from Miss Nancy's past.

EXTENSION

Students brought in other objects that Wilfred might have given to Miss Nancy, and developed a story to accompany each object. Stories were either written, told, or dramatized.

4. Interview

CONTEXT

In order to investigate the people who are a part of Miss Nancy's past, students interviewed peers who role played family members, friends, and people in the community who might have known her. Some of the roles were based on characters from the book, for example, Mrs. Jordon and Mr. Hosking, and others were invented, for example, her sister and her employer.

ACTIVITY

Students prepared a list of questions about Miss Nancy that they wanted answered. Questions were based on the characters in the story, the objects that Wilfred brings to Miss Nancy, and the information students had learned about Miss Nancy from Mem Fox 's book or from the drama. Once questions were prepared, students brainstormed a list of characters they wanted to interview. This was done in pairs and in small groups.

Students interviewed Miss Nancy (I played Miss Nancy). Because her memory wasn't clear, I was vague in my answers. This led to further questioning and encouraged interviewing among other characters.

5. Tableaux

CONTEXT

Photographs are a suitable context for depicting significant moments of a person's life. To help Miss Nancy recover her memory, students created a photo album that represented recollections that she might have preserved.

ACTIVITY

Students worked to create photos that might appear in Miss Nancy's photo album. They arranged the photos to reflect her life, and gave them captions to further create the image.

EXTENSION

Students chose one of the photos. They investigated by adding thought tracking, creating an improvisation of the moment, and telling the story as if on a silent videotape.

6. Art

CONTEXT

Students visually represented one of Miss Nancy's bedrooms in order to provide a reference point for ideas they discussed.

ACTIVITY

Students worked in small groups to create a collective drawing that represented a room from Miss Nancy's past. They decided at what stage in her life the room would represent. As students added furniture, books, photographs, and other mementos to the room, they gave a reference point for Miss Nancy's story and built a context for learning about her past.

EXTENSION

In addition to building a room, students created a significant photograph from Miss Nancy's album that reflected the same time period as that depicted in the room.

7. Writing

Students created a mailbox for Miss Nancy. This was a suitable context for sending letters to her in role of friends, neighbors, and family members.

ACTIVITY

Students brainstormed a list of reasons someone might write, or might have written, to Miss Nancy. They worked alone and in pairs to create mail that Miss Nancy would have received.

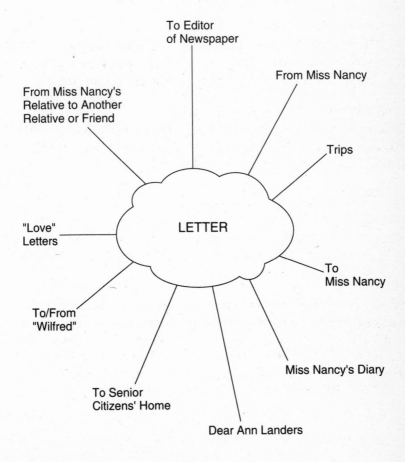

Writing in-role opportunities for this dramatheme

These pieces of writing helped to build an account of Miss Nancy's life. Using the information from the letters, students:

- role played interviews,
- wrote Miss Nancy in role, and responded as Miss Nancy to the letters,
- used significant statements from the letters in drama.

EXTENSION

Students investigated other forms of writing that gave evidence for Miss Nancy's life.

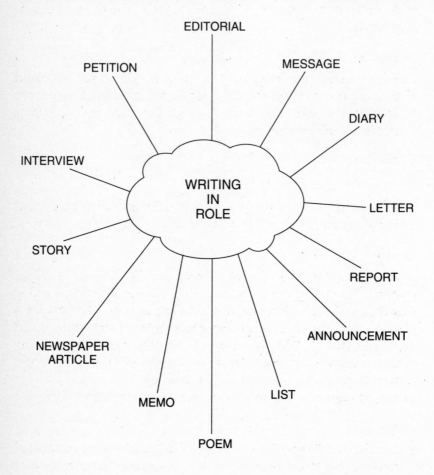

Writing genres that may be introduced at any time in a drama unit

8. Movement

CONTEXT

Miss Nancy's memories do not appear to be accurate. Using movement, students represented the distorted and abstract quality of these images.

ACTIVITY

Students created some of the dreams that Miss Nancy might have had that would recreate memories of her past. They chose to prepare these dreams in slow motion and mime. Sound, music, and voice-over narration accompanied these movement sequences.

EXTENSION

Groups created two images. One image (a still image but could also be a mime or short improvisation) depicted a moment from Miss Nancy's past. The second image depicted the way Miss Nancy remembers the incident.

9. Meeting

CONTEXT

In the picture book, Wilfred Gordon McDonald Partridge is faced with the problem of helping Miss Nancy recapture her memory.

ACTIVITY

Students worked in role to meet with the director of the senior citizens' home (I played the director). As the director, I called together several expert doctors to help me with Miss Nancy's case. During the meeting, the doctors (several students) raised questions that I could not answer. The doctors left the meeting and met with their cohorts (remaining students) to brainstorm answers to some of these questions. Students then met as a large group to compare the results of their brainstorming session.

EXTENSION

As an alternative problem-solving situation, students conducted a meeting that took place prior to Miss Nancy's admission to the senior citizens' home. Students role played family members who agreed to meet with the staff of the home to ask questions and seek advice.

10. Reflection

Students imagined that Miss Nancy had passed away. They decided to create a moment of Miss Nancy's funeral.

ACTIVITY

A table was used to represent Miss Nancy's coffin. Various people from Miss Nancy's past gathered to honor her. On a signal, each person shared his or her memory of Miss Nancy. Some were happy, others were sad. Several students chose to read part of a eulogy they wrote for her.

EXTENSION

Working alone, students created a still image that represented a moment from Miss Nancy's life and which honored her memory. As I tapped each person on the shoulder, she or he spoke one line that supported the image.

Beyond the Drama

Photographs

Students bring in a photograph or draw an illustration that represents an important memory or episode in their life. They use these pictures or drawings as a springboard for writing a memory story. In their stories, students describe when the event took place, who was there, how they felt, and why it was important. Once completed, these memory stories and pictures are displayed in an album for others to view and read.

Class Memories

One way to have students reflect upon important moments in the school day is to have them keep a timeline. On the timeline, they record specific incidents that made a day memorable. By taking a few moments at the end of the day, students can suggest items that might go on the class timeline. It might be interesting to have the students revisit the timeline at the end of each week or month. At the end of the year, students can revisit the timeline to recall incidences that added to or detracted from their class experience.

Family Treasures

In most families, photographs, books, scrapbooks, toys, pieces of clothing, jewelry, or art are important family treasures. Sometimes these treasures are passed on from generation to generation. As a class, arrange a storytelling session where students share some important family treasures. It might be possible for them to bring their treasures to class to accompany their storytelling, or they can draw the object. Students create a "memory museum" by displaying class mementos or drawings. They write a short description that tells the story and significance of each treasure.

Personal Timelines

As a means of revisiting important moments in their lives, students create a timeline. The timeline (I used strips of adding machine paper), comprises succinct notes on important events in their lives. Students will likely list events chronologically from birth to present. In events where they cannot remember when the incident occurred, they can list the time as approximate. For this activity, students consider:

• date and place of birth,
• prizes and awards,
• accidents,
• times they've moved,
• vacations,
• family births and deaths,
• special birthdays,
• clubs or teams they've joined,
• embarrassing moments,
• illnesses.

Once they have completed their timelines, students form small groups to share memories. As a group, they select one moment and write a collaborative story that explores the significance of the moment.

Interviewing an Adult

Students conduct an interview with a parent, relative, neighbor, or community member to discover special memories they recall from the past. If possible, a buddy arrangement could be made between the students and residents of a senior citizens' home. Prior to the interview, students prepare a list of questions they think might be interesting to find out about someone's past. Such topics as entertainment, school, moving, jobs, travels, awards or prizes, clubs, or organizations could be discussed in the interview. Each student taperecords his or her interview and shares it with others. Alternatively, students transcribe the interview and write an article about someone's past.

Memory Maps

This activity is similar to creating a timeline, but instead of using words to indicate important events and relationships, students prepare visual images that represent a "map" of their life. Students draw images, people, objects, or symbols that represent memories. Though some writing may appear on these maps, it should be limited to single words or phrases. Students should feel encouraged to interpret the word "map" in any way. Some will represent images to indicate a journey, others will represent individual scenes to create a storyboard sequence of events. Students may wish to use magazine photos and captions to create a collage that represents their life.

Retelling in Role

The class is divided in two sections. Students in the first section imagine that they are a character in a novel or picture book who is about to be interviewed on his or her life events. Students in the second section are magazine and newspaper reporters who will conduct the interview and discover the character's greatest life moments. Students from the first section find a partner from the second section. The reporter conducts his or her interview and transcribes it for the character's approval. When finished, students reverse roles.

Note: Any of the activities in this section can be conducted in role.

Assessment: Focus on Participation

Name: _____ Date: _____

Does the student:	Always	Sometimes	Never
1. Focus attention on the task at hand?	☐	☐	☐
2. Follow instructions effectively?	☐	☐	☐
3. Contribute ideas when planning?	☐	☐	☐
4. Revise and shape ideas for presentation?	☐	☐	☐
5. Accept different points of view?	☐	☐	☐
6. Collaborate in a variety of group situations?	☐	☐	☐
7. Appear to enjoy the drama?	☐	☐	☐

Comments:

_____

_____

_____

_____

_____

_____

_____

_____

_____

_____

_____

_____

_____

6/Folklore

"Even the wolf has a mother."

from "Into the Woods"

· · · · ·

Focus: Folktale, Fairy Tale

Once upon a time, the fairy tale was born. As these tales passed from generation to generation, some details were added, some were forgotten, and some were changed. In this dramatheme, students become part of this storytelling tradition as they go into the woods, make a wish, or discover the world that takes place in and beyond "happily ever after."

Learning Opportunities

- To use imagination and creativity to solve problems
- To identify and explore the basic plot and central problem(s) of fairy tales
- To practise playing the roles of characters in a story to better understand their thoughts, feelings, and motives
- To develop oral and written storytelling skills by elaborating and inventing stories within familiar tales
- To compare versions of a familiar fairy tale

Games: Focus on Imagination

Drawing Game

This activity provides students with the opportunity to demonstrate effective oral communication skills by giving and following directions accurately. To begin, students find a partner and sit back to back.

With paper and pencil, one student begins by drawing a simple picture such as the one shown above. She or he then gives directions that will allow the partner to duplicate the picture. To make the activity easier, listeners may be allowed to question their partners. To make the activity more difficult, instructions for more intricate designs can be given and no questions be allowed. At the end of the activity, partners compare their creation with the original design.

EXTENSIONS

- Students make up their own designs and, rather than give oral instructions, write accurate directions for others to follow.
- Partners take turns giving instructions regarding what to draw (e.g., draw a large circle in the centre of the page, then put three vertical stripes in the centre and add an eye on top of the circle). After each instruction, both partners draw what has been requested. Each partner gives eight to ten instructions. At the end of the activity, students compare their drawings to determine their success in giving and/or following directions.

Team Work

Students work in groups of four, six, or eight players. Within each group, players divide themselves into Team One and Team Two. Each team prepares a list. List A contains the names of animals and people. List B contains the names of objects. Alternatively, a list such as the one shown here is presented to the class as a model.

List A	List B
lawyer	match
dentist	crayon
alligator	microphone
pilot	calculator
raccoon	bottle
clown	stapler
baby	apple
mosquito	cactus
surgeon	penny
enemy	map

In each group, Team One and Team Two face each other. One person from Team One begins by saying, "What can a/an _____ (word from List A) do with a/an _____ (word from List B)?" or "Why does a/an _____ (word from List A need a/an _____ (word from List B)?" Team Two must find three answers within one minute. Team Two then takes a turn to pose a similar question to Team One. Once words have been used, they are crossed off the list. The game ends when all words have been used.

EXTENSIONS

- Each team gives as many answers as possible within one minute. Teams score a point for each answer.
- To make the game more complicated, a third column – places – is added. Numbers of teams remain the same, however, a sample question would be, "Why does a/an _____ (word from List A) need a/an _____ (word from List B) in _____ (word from List C)?"

If I Could Be...

This activity helps students to think about who they are, what they would like to be, and what they want to do. The following statements could be written on the board, or on a worksheet. Students fill in their answers before sharing them with others.

If I could be an animal, I'd be a(n) _____ because _____ .
If I could be a color, I'd be _____ because _____ .
If I could be a famous person, I'd be _____ because _____ .
If I could be a song, I'd be _____ because _____ .
If I could be a food, I'd be a(n) _____ because _____ .
If I could be a piece of furniture, I'd be a(n) _____ because _____ .
If I could be a musical instrument, I'd be a(n) _____ because _____ .
If I could be a shape, I'd be _____ because _____ .
If I could be a flower, I'd be a(n) _____ because _____ .

Other possibilities include: car, building, tree, word, country, insect, number, body of water, and flavor.

Note: This activity could be shared with younger children by giving them a choice, for example, "Would you rather be a robin, an elephant, or a cat?" and "Would you rather be an ocean, a river, or a lake?"

Dramatic Activities: Focus on Storytelling

Believe It or Not!

Students are given three blank file cards. On one card, they record a fact about themselves, for example, an accomplishment, a memorable incident from their life, or a hobby. Students should be cautioned that statements they record should be facts that can be shared with others. On the other two cards, students record two statements that sound true but are false. Students work in pairs. Each partner guesses which statement is true. They repeat the activity with several partners. Students choose one of their three statements. Working with a new partner, they interview each other about the incident, perhaps assuming the role of a reporter for Ripley's "Believe It or Not." Each partner should be prepared to answer any questions concerning their statement. At the end of the interview, students decide if the story their partner told was true or false.

EXTENSIONS

- Students work in groups of six to eight. They close their eyes while one person is chosen (silently, perhaps by a tap on the shoulder) to be the "true" storyteller. Other students work with their two false statements or make up new statements. Each person, in turn, reveals their statement to the other members of the group. Only one person will be telling the truth – the others will try to convince the group that they are the true storyteller. Group members discuss who they think is telling the truth. The game could also be played with the whole class.
- Students create a Ripley's "Believe It or Not!" newspaper by writing a short article that features one of the tall tale incidents they described in the storytelling sessions.

Story Wheel

This activity promotes listening skills and collaboration. Students lie on their backs and make a wheel formation, that is, their heads face in to the centre. One person is chosen to begin the story. Each person, in turn, adds to the collaborative story. The following statements are possible beginnings for the storytelling session:

- It was a dark and stormy night...
- Long ago, in a kingdom far away...
- Once, on the shores of a sea, a strange bottle was found...
- He was always told to stay away from the door, but one day...
- With a rub of the lamp, the genie was at last released...
- Until today, everyone laughed at the idea of a time machine...
- Once upon a time...

EXTENSION

- Students contribute to the story by saying "Freeze." They continue the story until someone interrupts them with a "Freeze" command. The person who interrupts then makes his or her contribution to the story.

Heroes and Villains

In small groups, students brainstorm fairy tale characters that they list under the following headings: animal characters, female characters, and male characters. When finished, members review their list to determine whether the characters are heroes or villains – they put an "H" beside the names of characters who are heroes and a "V" beside the names of characters who are villains.

Students pick a character they would like to role play. With a partner, they discuss each character's upcoming appearance on a television talk show. They decide if the character will be on the night the host invites heroes to appear, or the night the host invites villains to appear. Students briefly discuss questions a host might ask to discover the "true" story of the character. They take turns role playing the character and the television host.

Paired Improvisations Were Successful – Now What?

The following outline details strategies to be employed after paired improvisations such as those described previously. These strategies are particularly useful if students are working in the context of media reports.

1. Reporters stand. They report what they heard to the teacher in role as interviewer.
2. Storytellers stand. They report their story to the teacher in role as interviewer.
3. Storytellers stand. They find a new partner to whom they tell their story. The new partner now becomes the interviewer.
4. Storytellers or reporters, or both, conduct a meeting to share stories, for example, a press conference, an editorial meeting, or a city council meeting.
5. Storytellers and reporters form partners. They create a tableau image that encapsulates a story that was told. Two additional tableaux can show what happened before and what might happen next.
6. Partners enact the improvisation while audience members watch to learn new information about a character.
7. Partners switch roles and repeat the improvisation.
8. Partners switch tasks. The interview is conducted in some "future" time.

Extended Improvisation: Using a Fairy Tale – "Little Red Riding Hood"

In their book, *Stories in the Classroom*, David Booth and Bob Barton present four processes that have students work "Inside Outside and All Around the Story" (1990, p. 96).

1. Interpreting the Story (sharing what we have beheld)
2. Elaborating the Story (building on the story's strengths)
3. Extending the Story (stretching the tale)
4. Inventing from the Story (creating old from new)

The following outline provides students with the experience of exploring a familiar folktale using these four processes:

PROCESS	FUNCTION		POSSIBLE ACTIVITIES
INTERPRETING THE STORY	• express personal images and group images	TABLEAU	• create a frozen image to show the most exciting moment • add a scene before or after the image
	• review plot	STORY-TELLING	• retell the events of a story from a character's point of view
	• depict narrative, images, and dialogue	IMPROVI-SATION	• enact a one-minute scene that demonstrates the dilemma/problem of the story
ELABORATING THE STORY	• build on the story using questions children might have	QUES-TIONING	• as media reporters what students might want to find out
	• look for hidden truths	INTERVIEWING	• interview teacher in role as one who knows/might know • interview a character to find out the "true" story (pairs, small groups)

PROCESS	FUNCTION		POSSIBLE ACTIVITIES
ELABORATING THE STORY *(cont'd.)*	• look for hidden truths *(cont'd.)*	INTER-VIEWING	• hot-seating to explore actions, behaviors, feelings
	• burrow into story to discover its theme	DANCE/DRAMA	• list words that express story's themes and create a dance drama movement (or dream) to express those themes
EXTENDING THE STORY	• explore what might have happened, or could happen before or after the story	IMPROVI-SATION	• improvise a scene to show what might happen at some past or future point in time
	• explore stories within stories	STORYTELLING IN ROLE	• brainstorm, in pairs, small groups, or as a whole class, a list of characters who could be telling the tale
	• work in role to experience problem in the story or explore unresolved issues	MEETING	• whole group meets in role to discuss alternatives/solutions to a problem
INVENTING FROM THE STORY	• place characters in different situations from those mentioned in story by changing setting and/or time	WORKING WITH SET	• create a "set" for action to take place • improvise a scene to show how roles, languages, and problem would be different
	• use story concepts and patterns to create a new version	WRITING	• invent new characters, setting, time period, and dialogue to write a story patterned on the original
	• create a new story modeled on old by changing art form	PRESENT-ING	• Puppet presentation • Mime play • Videotape • Story Theatre

In his popular picture book *The True Story of the Three Little Pigs*, the author Jon Scieszka, writing as "A. Wolf" claims that "nobody knows the real story because nobody has ever heard *my* side of the story."

The framework that Scieszka uses for telling a traditional tale from another point of view ideally compliments one of the strongest goals of drama, namely to examine truths from other points of view. Because it provides an accessible context (newspaper report), demonstrates point of view, and provides invented storytelling, Scieszka's book is a gift to drama teachers to use as a model for elaborating, extending familiar tales, and inventing new versions. If we can interview the wolf who tempted three pig brothers, why not a wicked witch, a jealous step-sister, a giant in the sky, or perhaps another wolf who lured a girl in a red cape? The following outline demonstrates this strategy.

Phase One: Recalling Events from a Familiar Story (Interpreting)

Children sat in a circle to retell the events of a story with which they were familiar. Each student, in turn, contributed to the storytelling by adding a detail, a description, or a piece of information from the previous storyteller.

Phase Two: Storytelling in Role (Interpreting and Elaborating)

Students listened to James Marshall's picture book version of *Little Red Riding Hood*. Students compared Marshall's version to the one that was just told co-operatively. The storytelling activity was repeated with the students telling the story from the point of view of Little Red Riding Hood. Students were reminded to tell the story in the first person.

Phase Three: Looking at the "Other Side of the Story" (Elaborating)

A discussion was held to speculate whether the "wolf" in the tale might tell the same story. In small groups, students told the story from the wolf's point of view. As wolf, each storyteller contributed to the storytelling. On another occasion, this activity was done in small groups with one student playing the wolf, who was subsequently interviewed by the media.

Phase Four: Preparing Questions to Elaborate the Story

In order to get the "real" story, it was decided that the wolf was to be put on trial. Students prepared a list of questions they would like to have asked as lawyers for the case. One group prepared a list of questions to ask Little Red Riding Hood; another group, a list of questions to ask the wolf.

Phase Five: Creating Tableaux to Explain Events in the Story (Extending)

It was decided that evidence would be needed in order to get to the "real" story. Each group created a tableau that would serve as a photograph to be used in the trial. One group showed a photograph that proved Little Red Riding Hood's innocence while a second photograph showed the wolf to be innocent.

Phase Six: Presenting Tableaux to Convince Others (Interpreting and Elaborating)

Groups shared "photographs" and interpreted each scene. Two groups worked to persuade others to see their point of view. Each group was instructed to identify one character who would be able to serve as a witness to the story (e.g., Red's mother, Red's best friend, the wolf's mother).

Phase Seven: A Meeting (Elaborating)

One person from each group came forward, in turn, as a witness prepared to tell the story she or he knew. The class served as detectives who were preparing for the trial.

Note: As outlined by Norah Morgan and Julianna Saxton in *Asking Better Questions* (1994), several role options are available to enhance questioning, namely: the absentee, the researcher, the interviewer, the media reporter, the policeman, the detective, the lawyer, and the devil's advocate.

Phase Eight: Problem Solving in Role (Elaborating)

The class decided to sentence the wolf, but first they had to capture him. When they reached his den, they met a gentle woman (teacher in role) who was concerned about the meanness of her teenage son – the wolf – who seemed to scare anyone he encountered. At home, he tended to be very helpful and had been kind to his mother since his father passed away. Had the visitors seen him? Did they have any advice? What could be done with bullies who want to terrify others? The children sat with the wolf's mother offering her advice on how to deal with her teenage son.

Phase Nine: Writing a New Version (Inventing)

Students were given the option of writing a new version of "Little Red Riding Hood" by:

- telling The True Story of Little Red Riding Hood by A. Wolf (modeled on Scieszka's book),
- reversing the tale to show that it was the wolf who was afraid of Little Red Riding Hood,
- writing an interview between the wolf from "Three Little Pigs" and the wolf from "Little Red Riding Hood,"
- changing the setting, time, and/or characters from the tale.

Phase Ten: Comparing Versions

The class worked in groups. Each group was given a version of "Little Red Riding Hood" to read. After reading their version, group members discussed how it was similar to or different from other versions with which they were familiar (see Recommended Books, pg. 149). Working in the jigsaw group method, new groups were formed and members discussed various versions of the tale comparing characters, problems, setting, illustrations, and style.

Beyond the Drama

The following twenty-five activities help students explore fairy tales through reading, writing, talk, drama, and art.

Drama

1. Retell a fairy tale in five frozen pictures.
2. Retell a fairy tale as a dance drama (movement only).
3. Prepare a tape-recorded interview with a fairy tale character.
4. Create a puppet play for younger children.
5. Improvise a scene to show what happens to a character's future.
6. Create a scripted version of a fairy tale.
7. Conduct a talk-show interview with fairy tale characters.
8. Create a game show where questions are asked about fairy tales.
9. Have a fairy tale party (consider costumes, food, entertainment).
10. Create a fairy tale museum.

Reading

11. Create a bibliography of fairy tale books.
12. Collect and compare several versions of one tale.
13. Compare two versions of a fairy tale.
14. Review a picture book version of a fairy tale.
15. Use a version of a fairy tale as Readers Theatre.

Writing

16. Write and publish a modernized version of a tale by changing the characters and setting.
17. Write the diary entry of a fairy tale character.
18. Write a letter to an advice columnist in role as a fairy tale character.
19. Create a fairy tale newspaper.
20. Retell the story in poetry form.

Art

21. Create a mask for a fairy tale character to be used in a Story Theatre presentation of a fairy tale.
22. Illustrate a scene from a fairy tale for a new published version of the tale.
23. Invent a wanted poster for a fairy tale character.
24. Create a sculpture of a fairy tale character.
25. Create a diorama that would represent the set of a fairy tale.

Assessment:
Focus on Storytelling Skills

Name: _____ Date: _____

Does the student:	Always	Sometimes	Never
1. Share personal stories?	☐	☐	☐
2. Enjoy inventing stories?	☐	☐	☐
3. Listen attentively to the stories of others?	☐	☐	☐
4. Seem aware of audience?	☐	☐	☐
5. Tell stories clearly with attention to sequence, character, and description?	☐	☐	☐
6. Demonstrate an ability to retell stories?	☐	☐	☐
7. Demonstrate an ability to tell a story in role?	☐	☐	☐
8. Use story effectively within the drama?	☐	☐	☐

Comments:

_____

_____

_____

_____

_____

_____

_____

_____

_____

_____

_____

7/Community

"For teachers and students alike... learning is most effective when it takes place in a community whose members carry out inquiries on topics to which they have a personal commitment and who engage in collaborative, critical, and constructive dialogue ... In such a community of inquirers, the roles of teacher and learner are interchangeable for all are learning and, at the same time, all are helping others to learn."

Gordon Wells, *Constructing Knowledge Together* (1992, p. 51)

. . . . .

Focus: Map

Whether we live in a small farming community or a large urban neighborhood, knowing the people around us makes us feel part of a society. By confronting some of the problems that a fictitious town might face, the students may be able to better understand the meaning of the word "community" as they work through this dramatheme.

Learning Opportunities
- To work co-operatively, to share ideas, and to trust oneself and others
- To create and interpret maps to convey information
- To invent a fictitious society and explore the issues and problems facing that society
- To identify and explore the various people and places that contribute to a community
- To select and develop a role in a problem-solving context

Games: Focus on Trust

Breaking through the Wall

This physical game promotes co-operation and trust. The whole class, with the exception of two players, forms a tight circle by linking arms. One player goes inside the circle; one player remains outside the circle. The object of the game is for the player outside the circle to break in, and the player inside the circle to break out. All players forming the circle or the wall attempt to stop them. The game continues until one of the players succeeds in breaking through the wall.

EXTENSIONS

- Students discuss the two players and the wall of humans. Why would someone want to break into the group? Why would another try to break free? They also consider the wall. What does it represent?
- As a class, students prepare an investigation of two players who want to break through the wall.

Count to Ten

This activity, which builds group interaction and concentration, is not as easy to play as it may seem. Students sit in a group, or arrange themselves in a circle. The object of the game is to have the group count from one to ten, with only one person calling a number at a time. Students are instructed to call out a number when they think it is appropriate. The game begins with a student calling out "One." When two players call out a number at the same time, the game starts again.

EXTENSIONS

- Students countdown from "Ten" to "Blastoff!"
- Students challenge themselves to count as high as possible.
- Students recite the alphabet.
- Students play games in pairs, then in smaller groups.

Bat Cave

The class stands in a large open circle. One student is chosen to be the "bat," and is subsequently blindfolded. Four or five students are chosen to be "moths." The remaining students in the circle form the walls of the cave. The object of the game is for the bat to catch, as silently as possible, a moth wandering about the cave. At any time, the bat calls out the word "Bat." The moths respond by saying "Moths." As the bat wanders around the inside of the circle, it might get too close to the wall. Students who are the cave wall call out "Cave." The closer the bat is to the wall, the louder the call. Once a moth is tagged, she or he changes place with someone from the circle. The bat, too, can change place with someone from the circle.

Dramatic Activities: Focus on Persuasion

A Colorful Discussion

Students, working in pairs or groups of three, are asked to think of a favorite color. They then try to persuade their partner or other group members that their color is better and more important than others mentioned. Students should be encouraged to use any argument or means of verbal persuasion to convince others of their point of view. The activity could be repeated with students working with different people, or other "favorite" colors. After the activity, students discuss methods used to persuade others to their point of view. Did they use examples? How did they appeal to their opponents' emotions? Was bribery or flattery used? Were they always on topic?

EXTENSIONS

- Students work in small groups to brainstorm as many words or phrases that they can think of that pertain to a particular color. Students write their points on a sheet of paper of the same color. They exchange their completed lists for review and revision.
- Students are asked to imagine that only one color can be left in the world. They repeat the argument of colors with each group trying to convince the others that their color should be the one remaining color.

Let's Not Argue

The following dialogue is presented to the students:

Let's not argue.
Who's arguing?

Students work with this dialogue in several ways. They should be encouraged to work spontaneously, taking no time to prepare.

1. In pairs, students practise ways of reading the two lines aloud. Each partner takes turns beginning the conversation.
2. Students discuss the reasons for the argument, including the people arguing and where the argument takes place.
3. Students prepare a scene that occurs before the dialogue.
4. Students prepare a scene that occurs after the dialogue.
5. Students exchange roles to experience the other person's point of view.

Introduce the dialogue shown below. This helps students to further develop their communication skills as they work with minimal scripts (see pg. 135 for more information). No time is given for preparation. Partners are encouraged to respond spontaneously by picking up cues from their partners.

I didn't do it.
Yes you did!

Are you sure?
Of course I'm sure!

Tell me the truth.
I am telling the truth!

Yes.
No.

To further develop the students' skills of argument and communication, they are assigned the following "givens" as they improvise scenes using the minimal scripts:

• both partners clasp wrists, or put their hands on each other's shoulders,
• the argument is carried out in mime only,
• both players argue without looking at one another,
• both players sit on their hands during the confrontation,
• both players are frozen in place, except for their mouths.

Try to See It My Way

Drama allows students to examine problems from several points of view. The following activity prepares students to work in a variety of role situations, and encourages them to argue from different perspectives. Students work in groups to discuss one of the following problems. On a signal, they are assigned new roles and continue the argument from the perspective of that person. Students might be asked to return to those roles during the discussion.

1. A new highway is about to be built:
- farmers whose fields will be destroyed
- city planners who must decide where to build the highway
- unemployed workers who will be hired to build the highway
- tenants of a building who will be left homeless when their building is torn down to make room for the highway
- conservationists
- politicians who want to be re-elected

2. A tool factory that is going on strike:
- employees who have worked all of their lives at the factory
- owners who must restrict their budgets
- clients who buy goods from the company
- workers who draw up a list of improvements
- safety inspectors who are dissatisfied with the factory

3. Landing on a new planet:
- aliens who discuss the arrival of new citizens
- doctors who monitor travelers' health
- reporters who will advise the world about the discovery
- farmers who are inspecting the growth potential of the new planet's soil
- space photographers who only have three pictures remaining in their film

EXTENSIONS
- Once students have experienced the various roles, they replay the situation with each person assuming a different role.
- Groups work together to prepare a whole-class drama where students deal with one issue. Each group presents different roles in order to fully examine the situation.

Extended Improvisation: Using Maps –
A Study of a Community

> Maps are a useful resource for initiating a drama activity as a focus for creating a fictitious setting, as a stimulus for inventing roles of residents living in that setting, and as a way to present, through diagrams, problems that may face a community. Similarly, maps can be prepared as part of the drama in order to reflect on experience and provide a symbolic representation of places, events, or periods of time.

Some resources, such as *As the Crow Flies* or *Shaker Lane*, provide maps that can be used as documents for drama extension. Students can also prepare a map of a community by creating a representation of a place they have read about in a story. Alternatively, students can invent a map and as an ensemble build a story, setting, and problem. The following outline represents my experience with this dramatheme with a group of grade five students.

1. Mapping to Create a Community

I began this theme by reading *The House that Jack Built*, a book by Ruth Brown that looks at how a town must deal with the problem of pollution. I then outlined to the students their task for this activity: to create a community that was being polluted by a factory. Taping a large sheet of mural paper to the wall, we created a map of the community. Students arbitrarily placed the factory in the centre of the community. The letter ''F'' and an outline of the building were drawn on the map.

Students, in turn, were given a chance to come up to the map and mark a spot to show where they lived, worked, played, or relaxed in the community. As they came up to mark their spots, I asked some questions to help them develop their roles (e.g., How long have you lived in the community? What do you like about living in this community?).

Each student added something to the map. Some students added monuments, parks, stores, or other points of interest. Once everyone had recorded their mark, they discussed as a large group what the map told them about the community.

Note: If you have a large class, ask students to work in pairs to put a mark on the map.

VARIATION

- If you use a real map (e.g., *As the Crow Flies*), students can work in small groups to discuss what information they know about the community by looking at the map. They could choose a place in the community to show where they might like to work or live. Students identify a role for themselves by marking an ''X'' or a dot on the map.

2. Interviewing to Develop Roles

Students worked in groups of three or four for the next part of the activity. One student assumed the role of a citizen while the other students played the role of tourists who came from another town, and who wanted the chance to speak with a resident about their life in the community. Prior to the meeting, the tourists used the information from the map to think of questions about the community that they would like to ask a resident. Once the interviews were finished, the tourists shared information they had learned about the community. In role as the mayor of their home town, I was given a summary of their findings.

3. Discussing the Problem in a Town Meeting (Teacher in Role)

When a teacher works in role, she or he adopts a set of attitudes to work with the students. While acting skill is not required, the teacher must alter his or her status in the classroom to help students explore issues or examine possible directions a drama may take. Depending on the role that the teacher takes, she or he can extend the drama, focus attention, challenge the class, suggest alternatives, support contributions, slow the action, and clarify information in order to enhance the commitment, the language, and the thoughts and feelings of students as they work in a fictional context.

TEACHER IN ROLE

ROLE	FUNCTION	SOME OPTIONS FOR TOWN MEETING
Narrator	• shares memories of incident(s) • summarizes events, or action of drama	• citizen who "remembers the time when. . ." • storyteller explaining incident about the building of the factory
Leader	• establishes conflict, dilemma, tension • challenges students to challenge, persuade, or resolve conflicts	• mayor of the community • boss/owner of the factory • head of environmental committee
Opposer	• challenges decisions • disbelieves to demand proof, facts • opposes to bring group together	• developer who wants to build in the community • union leader who wants to protect factory employees
Low-status	• elevates group's need to take responsibility • empowers	• factory employee • visitor to the community • potential immigrant
Messenger	• acts as intermediary • links authority and low-status roles • passes and/or receives information	• reporter seeking information • mayor's assistant who is compiling concerns
Shadow	• assists and side-coaches "in" the drama • shares commitment with children	• one of the concerned villagers • one who was born in the village long ago

To help the students consider the problem of the factory and the pollution it caused, I suggested holding a town meeting. In role as the citizens of the community, students gathered to discuss ways of dealing with the pollution. I assumed the role of assistant to the mayor. My role was to listen to the concerns and problems the citizens raised.

Students, still in role, met in small groups to come up with solutions of how to deal with the factory's emissions. I then assigned a role to each group. In their groups, students discussed the pollution issue from these viewpoints:

GROUP 1: the unemployed
GROUP 2: mayor's council from city hall
GROUP 3: board of directors and owners of the factory
GROUP 4: environmentalists
GROUP 5: citizens who have lived in the community their entire life

VARIATIONS

- Though the problem of the factory might be a central focus for exploration, other problems might be explored by the students, depending on what story you used to introduce the theme (e.g., an unwanted neighbor in *Old Henry*).
- Alternatively, students may suggest problems that a community encounters once they have deciphered and interpreted a map that was used to start the drama (e.g., unwanted visitors who want to move the community, a mean leader who controls the community).

4. Persuading through Writing

Students were given an opportunity to offer an opinion about what could be done to help solve the pollution problem. They chose one of the following contexts to persuade others to make changes:

- a letter to the mayor explaining how their life was affected by the decision to keep the factory in the community,
- an editorial published in the local newspaper persuading readers to see their point of view and to take action to improve the community,

- a petition to be drawn up and distributed among citizens that outlined community complaints, as well as a list of suggested solutions/demands,
- a report sent by the factory owners explaining reasons why the factory is beneficial to the community,
- a "paid political" announcement to be read over the radio that advises others to take action.

Once students had finished, they shared their writing at a press conference. Written pieces served as a stimulus for further discussion, argument, and persuasion. Students discussed a possibility of compromise and offered hypotheses about the future of the community.

5. Panel Discussion

I asked students to imagine that a local news show had been following the developments occurring in their community. Working in groups of five or six, students formed a panel and developed a presentation that was intended to convince others to accept their point of view. One student in each group role played the part of the interviewer and prepared questions to ask panel members. Discussions were videotaped and shown to others who served as the television audience. When each panel had shown their tape, a vote was held to determine the panel whose arguments were most persuasive.

Beyond the Drama

Alternate Mapping Activities

Students work in small groups to create a second map that depicts one of the following:

- an ideal community that has no factories,
- an industrialized community that has many new factories,
- a map of a community as it might appear in the future, (e.g., a century from now).

Back in Time

Students place themselves in the time of the 1920s. Their town council has just received a proposal to build a factory. Their town, which is close to a large lake, has prospered on the summer tourist trade. The factory would mean year-round work for the townspeople. Students write a letter to council outlining their support or protest of the factory proposal.

Creating Rules or Laws

By inventing rules or laws, students create a document that focuses attention on specific problems. They look at the necessity of such laws, what happens when they are broken, and what laws need to be modified to reflect changing times and attitudes.

Writing Letters

Students imagine that some people have chosen to move away from the community. They explore the scenario through hypothesizing about letters written by those who chose to stay in the community and those who chose to leave. In each instance, community members (past and present) justify their reasons for staying or leaving.

Assessment:
Focus on Problem-Solving Skills

Name: _____ Date: _____

Does the student demonstrate
an ability to:

	Always	Sometimes	Never
1. Communicate?	☐	☐	☐
2. Question?	☐	☐	☐
3. Argue?	☐	☐	☐
4. Persuade?	☐	☐	☐
5. Negotiate?	☐	☐	☐
6. Brainstorm?	☐	☐	☐
7. Hypothesize?	☐	☐	☐
8. Take risks?	☐	☐	☐
9. Collaborate?	☐	☐	☐
10. Reflect?	☐	☐	☐

Comments:

_____

_____

_____

_____

_____

_____

_____

_____

_____

_____

_____

_____

_____

8/The Past

"Theatre is the direct experience that is shared when people imagine and behave as if they were other than themselves in some other place at another time."

Jonothan Neelands, *Structuring Drama Work* (1990, p. 4)

. . . . .

Focus: Novel

What would happen if we could use today's knowledge and apply it to yesterday's news? Stories about history's pioneers and heroes have always intrigued us. As we come to understand what happened before we were born, we come to feel a part of the survival and quest of our ancestors. In this dramatheme, students look in history's rear-view mirror in order to be better prepared for the road ahead.

Learning Opportunities
- To develop concentration skills by focusing on specific issues
- To practise role playing in order to better understand the thoughts, feelings, and motivations of others
- To explore tension and dilemma by making decisions
- To examine the history of the Underground Railroad by working "as if"
- To research information arising from dramatic situations

Games: Focus on Concentration

One Potato, Two Potato

This activity promotes concentration and invites students to pay close attention to detail. Each student is given a potato (or oranges, rocks, or apples) to examine. They understand that they should know their potato so well that they would be able to identify it in a mass of potatoes. Students are not allowed to mark their potato in any way. Potatoes are placed in a pile and mixed – students must find their potato among the pile.

EXTENSIONS

- Students write a brief description of their potato. It should be detailed enough that someone might be able to identify the potato by its written description.
- Potatoes are displayed throughout the room. Descriptions are collected and distributed randomly throughout the class. Students are told that these descriptions have been filed with the police department under the missing potatoes files. Working in role as investigators, students try to find the missing potato by matching it with its description.

A Cat/A Hat

Once the students catch on to this game, it tends to be a favorite. To begin, the game is played in groups of eight to ten students. Eventually, the whole class plays the game. One person, perhaps the teacher, is Player One. This role demands some concentration, and the person playing this part is responsible for keeping the game going. The following script best demonstrates how the game is played:

Player One   (to Player Two):   I give you a hat.
Player Two   (to Player One):   A what?
Player One   (to Player Two):   A hat.
Player Two   (to Player Three): I give you a hat.
Player Three (to Player Two):   A what?
Player Two   (to Player One):   A what?
Player One   (to Player Two):   A hat.
Player Two   (to Player Three): A hat.
Player Three (to Player Four):   I give you a hat. . .

Once the game is underway, Player One turns to the player on his or her left saying, "I give you a cat." The cat segment is relayed simultaneously with the hat. At one point, a player will get the hat and the cat – the trick is to pass both on, in either direction. These words can be exchanged for other words, for example, bag-rag, and bone-stone. Sometimes players pass an object in either direction as they say their lines. This may simplify the game; at other times, it causes even more confusion!

Dramatic Activities: Focus on Role

Missing Person

This activity allows students the opportunity to use clothing and objects as a source for developing a character's identity. Students gather clothing from home or from the lost and found box (e.g., hats, scarves, an old coat, a sweater, or objects such as a box, a ribbon, a toy, jewelry). Students are told that these items were found in an abandoned apartment and are the only clues to the identity of a missing person. Students discuss what each object reveals about its owner. They brainstorm a list of words that describe the person, and offer suggestions about his or her background, based on clothing and objects found in the apartment.

EXTENSION

- Students suggest people who might know something about the missing person, and volunteer to role play these characters. In small groups or as a whole class, other students role play the part of investigators quizzing these people for clues to the missing person.

Who Am I?

This popular theatre game encourages student interaction and role building. To play this game, each student has a card pinned to his or her back that is prepared with the name of a celebrity, a historical figure, a book character, or a character from a nursery rhyme or fairy tale. Students must not know the name of the character printed on the card on their back.

The object of the game is for players to find out who they are by asking other players questions about their character that can be answered with a "Yes" or "No" response. They are allowed to ask one question per player. Once players have guessed their identities, they pin their card to their front. They continue to answer questions for players who have yet to discover the identity of their character.

- Students assume the identity of their character. With a partner, they improvise one of the following situations:
  - a job interview
  - an interview with an entertainment magazine
  - a telephone conversation
  - a conversation between seat companions on a train trip
  - meeting people at a wedding or funeral of a mutual friend
- Players, assuming the identity of their character, role play taking part in a bridge game with three other players who are also in role. In their groups of four, players decide what their characters have in common.
- As a class, discuss which characters would form the best foursome for bridge.

A Day in the Life

This is a useful strategy to use in drama, particularly when a character is faced with a problem she or he must solve. This activity helps students recognize the roles we assume in various situations. The activity can be played in pairs or in small groups. One person should be assigned the central role; his or her partner or group members will switch roles throughout the improvisation. The following scenarios are outlined to the students. They choose one to improvise:

Teenager
- eating breakfast with his or her family
- meeting friends at school
- discussing lackadaisical work habits with his or her teacher(s)
- applying for an after-school job
- meeting his girlfriend's or boyfriend's parents

Parent

— eating breakfast with his or her family
— asking his or her boss for a raise
— sitting in the cafeteria with his or her friends
— meeting a son's or daughter's teachers
— discussing a broken curfew with a son or daughter

Teacher

— discussing a headache in the staffroom
— talking to the principal about lack of supplies
— shopping for a gift for his or her parent
— speaking to a student about his or her behavior
— talking to a professor about a poor grade she or he received on an essay

After experiencing one of the situations, students discuss how we change roles according to who we are with and where we interact. As well, they discuss how the concept of self varies from situation to situation and how we use techniques to put other people at ease. Students can be asked to identify times when they feel most like themselves, and times when they feel least like themselves.

EXTENSION

• Students work in different groups. In each group, one member plays the same central character. This character meets different people throughout the day, and may discuss his or her problem with some or all of them.

Extended Improvisation: Using a Novel – *Underground to Canada*

The Underground Railroad, which was first documented in 1787, was a network of people and hiding places that helped slaves escape to Canada. One of the most famous freedom fighters was Harriet Tubman, who was born a slave in 1820. During her nineteen trips on the Underground Railroad, Harriet Tubman led over 300 slaves to freedom and never lost one person.

In this dramatheme, students explore a period in history to help them understand some of the realities of slavery and the celebration of freedom. By manipulating time, students will explore the preparations Harriet Tubman made before each journey, the difficulties faced in these journeys, and the liberation of the people she guided to Canada.

Several resources provide students with background narratives and information about the slaves' escape to freedom. In particular, Barbara Smucker's *Underground to Canada* is an excellent resource that draws on historical accounts of the Underground Railroad and Harriet Tubman's life. The story invites readers to use their imagination to recount aspects of slavery and is a suitable resource to introduce students to the topic by providing opportunities for drama exploration.

The activities described in this session, which have been organized into phases that represent four varieties of dramatic action, are based on Jonothan Neelands' book, *Structuring Drama Work*. As Neelands states, this conventions classification system is not intended to be hierarchical or sequential but has been developed "in response to certain basic needs required for participation, either as a spectator or as an actor in dramatic activity" (1990, pp. 6-7).

The following outline documents a drama structure I used with a grade six class after experiencing *Underground to Canada*. Prior to the drama, students reviewed and discussed information about slavery that they learned from this book.

Phase One: Context-Building Action

Conventions which set the scene or add information to the drama as it unfolds.

Collective Drawing

The act of creating a drawing helped students give form to characters and setting, and provided them with a common response to the historical period. In order to help students establish motives for slaves undertaking such an epic journey, I asked them to form two groups. One group created a drawing that represented places and circumstances that the slaves left. The second group created a drawing that represented what the slaves envisioned as their final destination and freedom.

Phase Two: Narrative Action

Conventions which tend to emphasize the story or what happens-next dimension of the drama.

A Day in the Life

In this drama, students experienced the dilemma that a slave would have faced in deciding whether to remain a slave or attempt the dangerous escape to freedom. To help students understand the inner conflicts and tensions that a slave would have experienced in making this decision, I asked students to work backward from the event – they had to fill in gaps of why and how slaves came to view a dangerous and possibly fatal journey over a life of slavery.

As a large group, students worked on a slave's decision to accept Harriet Tubman's proposal to escape. Forming smaller groups, they created scenes that showed a central character at various points during a twenty-four hour period that preceded "boarding" the Underground Railroad:

- an invitation to join the Underground Railroad,
- a meeting with friends and family members who are skeptical about the slave's chance to survive,
- a meeting with an elderly family member who cannot escape,
- a meeting with a slave owner,
- witnessing an event that depicts "the last straw" of injustice.

Students ordered their scenes to present a chronology of the twenty-four hour time period. Each group revised its work, taking into account the influence of other group's scenes. Once completed, scenes were shown and the students reflected on the experience by discussing factors that motivated a slave to make a choice.

Phase Three: Poetic Action

Conventions which emphasize or create the symbolic potential of the drama through highly selective use of language and gesture.

Re-enactment

Re-enactment allows students to inspect the details and authenticity of an event as they work to reveal what might have happened. For this activity, students reconstructed a moment that a slave might have experienced, including death, capture, close calls, or the making of alternate plans. To help the students discover the tension and authenticity of an incident, I asked them to form groups so that they could discuss a situation and prepare a "still image" that re-enacted such a moment.

Once students froze their action, they could, on a signal, speak aloud their private thoughts and reactions to the situation. This thought-tracking aspect of the activity helped students reflect on the action. Some students froze in order to tap for thoughts; others proceeded with the presentation of still images.

Phase Four: Reflective Action

Conventions which emphasize soliloquy or inner thinking in the drama, or allow groups to review the drama from within the framework.

Voices in the Head

> This strategy is useful in helping students reflect on the many facets a character in a drama must face in making a choice. Students represent the possible conflicting thoughts of the character at the moment the decision is made. The voices become the conscience of a character that gives the person advice, forcing him or her to make a moral or life-threatening choice.
>
> This strategy helps the students to become more aware of the complexity of a problem, and allows them to influence the imminent action. As students call out their thoughts, they slow down the action of the drama, adding tension to the moment.

In Faith Ringgold's picture book, it is Aunt Harriet's voice that "came like a gust of wind sending messages, lullabies, and warnings" to Cassie as she seeks her brother. Aunt Harriet's "voices in the wind" is an ideal context for exploring reflection in this drama.

Ringgold writes about a real "train in the sky" that took slaves to freedom. Students explored the pressures that might have caused a young slave to leave his or her "home" by depicting the thoughts and conscience that Cassie (or another slave) might have experienced. One student took the role of Cassie as she is on the train. The rest of the group spoke to her as the voice of her family, friends, slave owners, former slaves, and slaves who had already joined the Underground Railroad.

Note: By "creating" the train, students have a richer opportunity for creating "context-building action."

Beyond the Drama

Researching Slavery

Students investigate other people who played a part in helping slaves escape to freedom. In particular, *Many Thousand Gone* by Virginia Hamilton is a valuable resource for this activity.

1. John Fairfield who posed as a slave trader
2. Thomas Garret, a Quaker who ran a comfort station in Delaware
3. William Still, a coal merchant, free-born in Pennsylvania
4. Levi Coffin, a Quaker who helped more than 3000 slaves escape
5. Susan B. Anthony, a runaway slave
6. Frederick Douglass, a runaway slave who assisted others in making the last "jump" to Canada

Once students gather information, they prepare a monologue that informs others of this person's story. Students read these monologues aloud in the role of the historical figure, and a press conference is held where other students question these historical figures about their experiences.

Art: Images of Slavery

At the time of slavery, there was a law that forbade slaves to learn to read or write (see *Nightjohn* by Gary Paulsen). For this activity, students imagine that the slaves have created drawings in order to depict their experiences and feelings. In role, they illustrate incidents that might have happened to slaves, and dreams and nightmares they might have experienced.

The finished drawings are put up on display as a museum exhibition focusing on slavery. Students examine one another's drawings in order to interpret the story behind each picture.

Freedom Songs

Students learn and sing several songs and spirituals that the slaves sang during their escape to freedom (see *Gonna Sing My Head Off: American Folk Songs for Children*). As an extension, students create verses for the songs "Follow the Drinking Gourd" and "Michael Row Your Boat Ashore," two songs about slaves and freedom.

Documenting of Slavery Experiences: Writing in Role

In 1869, Harriet Tubman's autobiography *Scenes in the Life of Harriet Tubman* was dictated to Sarah Bradford. In 1886, a revised edition was published under the title: *Harriet: The Moses of the People*.

Because of the literacy law, there is limited written documentation of people's experience of traveling the Underground Railroad. Once slaves arrived in Canada, however, propose to students that they might have had the chance to dictate their stories to those who were able to read and write.

In order to prepare a historical document of the Underground Railroad, students conduct in-role interviews between slaves and writers. When transcribing the interview, students consider moments of tension, sadness, joy, and bravery slaves experienced on their journey. Rather than transcribing their interview, some students may choose to share their learning through poems, letters, diary entries, and drawings – all of which are included in the historical document.

Preparing a Documentary

Preparing a documentary allows students to examine a theme, issue, or story from different viewpoints using a variety of drama conventions. As they work in groups to prepare a documentary, students examine material and thus come to understand the power of using the media to inform or persuade audiences about a topic. When dealing with historical or news events, students have the opportunity to gather, interpret, and deliver information at both a personal and societal level.

Students can prepare a documentary on "The History of the Underground Railroad." They discuss material and strategies they will incorporate into their documentary. One member can videotape the group's documentary so that it can be shown to others. Students consider the following points:

- people to be interviewed,
- storytellers,
- narrators,
- presentation method,
- written work to be presented (e.g., letters, lists, diaries),
- artifacts to be shown (e.g., maps, clothing, mementos),
- use of tableaux,
- incorporation of art in the presentation,
- use of movement,
- music.

Poetry

Eloise Greenfield's poem "Harriet Tubman" relates Harriet's story in verse. In small groups, students read and discuss the poem before preparing a choral dramatization. When they are satisfied with their presentation, they use the poem's rhyme scheme to write another verse about Harriet Tubman's achievements and bravery. Each group tape records their presentation, including the new verse. They may then decide to accompany the recording with a tableau or movement piece. Groups decide on the strategy they will pursue. They practise and refine their movements to ensure that they support the poem's mood and intent. When all groups have finished their work, they share it with others in the class.

VARIATION

- A useful activity for choral speaking is to combine a poem such as "Harriet Tubman" with another text, for example, Martin Luther King's speech, "I Have a Dream." This can be done by using one or two lines from one text, then alternating with one or two lines from the second text.

Harriet Tubman didn't take no stuff

I am happy to join you this day in what will go down in history as the greatest demonstration for freedom in the history of our nation. . .

Assessment:
Focus on Role-Playing Skills

Name: _____ Date: _____

Does the student:	Always	Sometimes	Never
1. Recognize the difference between working in role and working as self?	☐	☐	☐
2. Use language, gesture, and props appropriate to the role?	☐	☐	☐
3. Understand and identify with attitudes of the role?	☐	☐	☐
4. Recognize and accept the roles of others?	☐	☐	☐
5. Recognize and is committed to the intent of the drama?	☐	☐	☐
6. Explain, question, and challenge in role?	☐	☐	☐
7. Develop a character to build the drama?	☐	☐	☐
8. Accept the teacher in role within a drama?	☐	☐	☐
9. Reveal ideas and feelings in role through talk?	☐	☐	☐
10. Reveal ideas and feelings in role through writing?	☐	☐	☐

Comments:

_____

_____

_____

_____

_____

_____

_____

9/The Future

"On the one hand drama allows students to reflect on their experience, and on the other drama provides the opportunity to speculate on experience by asking: What would happen if the world were not as it is?"

John McLeod, *Drama Is Real Pretending* (1988, p. 96)

. . . . .

Focus: Poem

Only in drama can we turn the clock forward and make tomorrow come to life. Because no one can really see into the future, the students' ideas about tomorrow may be as real as those of scientists or the person sitting beside them. In this dramatheme, the students are invited to make predictions about life in the future, and share their concerns about a universe we do not yet understand.

Learning Opportunities
- To make predictions about life in the future
- To negotiate with others by playing games and participating in activities that involve collaboration and decision making
- To develop improvisation skills by working in fictitious situations
- To participate as experts by working in role as those who know
- To demonstrate the willing suspension of disbelief to travel to any place in any time

Games: Focus on Negotiation

Word Power

Students are asked to imagine that a wizard is about to take away all the words they know with the exception of three words of their choice. They record these words on a piece of paper. Students then use their three words to communicate with a partner. (They can also use gestures and mime.) To continue the activity, the wizard allows partners to share words so that each student adds three new words to his or her paper. Students find new partners and communicate with the six words on their list. The activity continues with students changing partners several times.

EXTENSION

- Students work in groups of six or eight. Members of each group decide on the words they would keep if the word wizard dictated that they could have only a ten-word vocabulary. As a whole-group activity, students decide on the ten words they think are essential for communication.

Elevens

Students sit in groups of three. Players chant "North/South/East/West," which is the signal for each member of the group to show any number of fingers from one hand. They count the total number of fingers shown. A closed fist counts as zero. The object of the game is for the group to show a total of eleven fingers. Players cannot confer with one another. As a competition, the first team to complete the task successfully five times, or the team with the most number of successful completions within a given time limit can be declared the winner.

EXTENSION

- Players use both hands. The object is to show twenty-three fingers.

Mixed Messages

This co-operative learning strategy helps students to learn about negotiation and communication at the same time that it allows for observation of students' collaborative skills. Players work in groups of five. Each group receives five envelopes (one envelope per person). If a group has less or more than five players, it should still be given five envelopes. Cut-up words in the envelopes are:

Envelope #1: vacation John the coyotes
Envelope #2: lunch Jessica howled night the
Envelope #3: it's our present dashed I wind
Envelope #4: through think time soon a
Envelope #5: forest for gave all the starts

On a signal, players open their envelopes and display the words in front of them. As a group, they construct five complete sentences from the five envelopes. They must follow these rules as they work:

• No one may speak.
• No one may signal for a word.
• Words must be given from one player to another. A player is not allowed to reach over and take a word from another player's envelope.

Sample sentences that can be formed from these words include:

1. Our vacation starts soon.
2. I think it's time for lunch.
3. The wind howled all night.
4. The coyotes dashed through the forest.
5. Jessica gave John a present.

Once players in each group have made five sentences from the words, they discuss how they felt about the activity, including how it felt to help someone, how it felt to be helped or not helped, and how this activity increased their understanding of co-operation.

Note: Older students can prepare their own five-word sentences for this activity. Once they have completed the sentences, they write each word they used on separate pieces of paper. They divide the words among five envelopes and give them to another student so that she or he can make sentences from the words. Students compare the sentences they created.

- Players are allowed to speak. They work with lines of a poem. Each group rearranges the lines into what players think is the correct order.

Face to Face?

This is an alternative structure for students to role play a conflict situation. Students form two lines, with each student facing a partner. Students in one line assume the identity of "A"; students in the other line assume the identity of "B." Partners are assigned a conflict situation and a point of view. On a signal, each pair discusses the issue according to their roles. On another signal, students reverse roles to understand the other person's point of view. After a few moments, the students switch roles again.

"A" wants to see a funny movie/"B" wants to see a horror movie.

"A" wants to play baseball/"B" wants to play a board game.

"A" wants to eat pizza/"B" wants to eat hamburgers.

"A" wants to vacation in the city/"B" wants a beach vacation.

"A" has a secret/"B" tries to get "A" to tell the secret.

"A" wants to borrow "B's" homework/"B" refuses.

"A" finds $10 and wants to spend it/"B" wants to find the owner.

"A" recycles garbage/"B" doesn't.

"A" thinks watching television is a waste of time/"B" is a television addict.

EXTENSION

- On a signal, students in one line shift direction so that they have a new partner. They repeat one of the above situations and/or reverse roles.

Note: This structure is useful to use in drama as an alternate way of working in pairs. Students can discuss ways that their classmates played the same role, and review arguments that they used to express a point of view.

Dramatic Activities:
Focus on Improvisation

Travel Time

"Oh, a time machine will never work -
You cannot solve its mystery.
"So step right in," the professor said.
"When this button's pressed, you'll be history!"

"History be you'll, pressed button's this when.
Said professor the, "in right step so"
Mystery its solve cannot you.
Work never will machine time a, Oh"

L.S.

Students read the poem to themselves before reading it aloud with a partner. They discuss questions they have about the poem and then improvise a scene between the professor and his "guinea pig." Who might be interested in entering the time machine? What questions might someone have before pressing the button? Will the professor convince someone to actually enter the time machine?

Partners reverse roles. In this improvisation, the professor is selective about who he will allow in to his time machine. What qualifications might this person need? How convincing must the applicant be in order to persuade the professor to let him or her use the machine?

Partners join with another set of students. Together, in groups of four, they discuss what might happen once the "button" is pressed. They create an image to show the period in the future that the time travelers have entered. Groups show one another their scenes as evidence that they have visited the future. Audience members ask questions in the role of the professor and his assistants who wish to know the success of the mission.

Machines

This popular movement activity has students use their bodies to express ideas and collaborate to make a creation. Students are told that they are going to create a time machine. The activity begins when one student makes a repetitious movement that represents one part of a machine's engine. One by one, others join in, attaching themselves to the first person and to one another in some way. Each person, in turn, adds a movement. The activity continues until the entire group is connected and moving. On a signal, each person adds a sound to accompany his or her movement.

EXTENSION

- The activity could be repeated in small groups with each group creating a machine for the future that creates a product or performs some sort of function beneficial to humans.

Inventors and Inventions

Using found materials, students work in small groups to create a time machine that could be used as a set for the drama. Groups decide whether the machine travels to the past, the future, or both. Once completed, machines can be featured at an inventors' competition. Each group should be prepared to explain how their machine works and answer questions from fellow inventors.

Extended Improvisation: The Future

Often teachers, particularly those who are involved with rotary, are faced with the dilemma of structuring a drama unit when they are only given short blocks of time.

The following timetable outlines my experience with a unit on time travel. The accompanying agenda outlines the lessons, which explored a different drama focus each day.

EPISODE ONE	EPISODE TWO	EPISODE THREE	EPISODE FOUR	EPISODE 5
9:00-9:45 About Time Travel	9:00-9:45 Designing a Time Machine	1:00-1:45 Mantle of the Experts	1:00-2:45 Preparing for the Mission	1:00-3:00 Into the Future
• discussion • paired improvisation • meeting	• group design • report in role as inventors	• meeting with teacher in role to get information • dance/drama • image of future	• farewells • small-group improvisation • meeting • Conscience Alley	• decision (how far in future) • problem (to stay in present or go to future)

Episode One: About Time Travel

Discussion

Students discussed, in small groups, questions such as the following:

- With what time-travel stories/movies are you familiar?
- Why would someone want to visit the future?
- What are some potential drawbacks of visiting the future?

Paired Improvisation

An inventor (Partner "A") created a time machine and was seeking applicants for "guinea pigs" (Partner "B") who might be somewhat skeptical about traveling to the future. The interview was replayed with partners switching roles. This time the applicant ("A") was eager to time travel but the inventor ("B") was reluctant to accept this person.

Meeting

In role as the time-traveler's assistant, I conducted a meeting with potential candidates. I listened to applicants, and answered their questions concerning the time-travel vehicle. Those who decided that they might like to try the machine attempted to convince doubters to join the mission by outlining the benefits of time travel.

Episode Two: Designing a Time Machine

Students worked in small groups. Using large sheets of paper, they worked as designers to create a blueprint drawing of a time machine. Students were encouraged to list materials, label different parts, and write instructions on how the machine worked. Two groups exchanged drawings. In role as inventors, members of each group questioned one another to find out how the machine functioned.

Episode Three: Mantle of the Expert

Meeting with Teacher in Role

Students were given the opportunity to become experts on time travel. The teacher, in role as a potential time traveler, sought advice from those who had gone before. A meeting was held where students role played characters who had returned from a time-travel mission. They described their trip – what they saw, how they felt, and what they learned.

The Mantle of the Expert

> When students wear "the mantle of the expert," characters in the drama have a special knowledge that is relevant to a situation. Mantle of the expert empowers the students and provides them with responsibility, information, and respect. For more about this topic see *Drama for Learning: Dorothy Heathcote's Mantle of the Expert Approach* (1995) by Dorothy Heathcote and Gavin Bolton.

Images of the Future

Students were told that previous time travelers had recorded their trip through the use of a video recorder. While they were able to capture one-minute scenes of the future, they could not tape the sounds they heard. In small groups, students prepared scenes of the future that they showed to potential space travelers. As well, they devised methods to let viewers know of the sounds they would experience through taping what previous visitors had heard.

Episode Four: Preparing for the Mission

In groups, students improvised a scene in which they told someone special in their lives about their mission. "Travelers" explained why they were going, what they hoped to see, and reported on their preparations for entering the time machine. Friends and family members had the option of being supportive or skeptical. Time travelers met and reported on what they had told their friends and families. They discussed their concerns and excitement about the mission.

Conscience Alley

> Jonothan Neelands and Tony Goode introduced me to this "Voices in the Head" strategy which is useful to make public some of the conflicts and dilemmas a character in a drama might

experience. The class forms two facing lines, thus forming an alley. The teacher (or student in role) represents a protagonist from the drama. As the character walks slowly down the alley, the students represent the character's conscience to show his or her thoughts about making a choice.

This strategy helped students inspect the thoughts a person might have about traveling to another time. Issues they looked at included: what the person will miss most about home, what his or her life will be like if a return trip home proves impossible, discoveries they may witness, and other questions – both factual and fanciful – about the mission.

Episode 5: Into the Future (double period)

Meeting to Negotiate and Make a Decision

Students discussed the time period they would like to visit. In a meeting of travelers, they voiced their opinions concerning the period they would visit.

Problem (with thanks to Cecily O'Neill)

After explaining to the group that they had traveled forty years into the future, I presented the following problem to the students:

The group returns back to the date of departure. Although the day is the same, forty years have passed and everyone they know has grown forty years older. The time travelers have not aged. Travelers meet with their friends and relatives to report on their mission and to learn how life has changed. They must now decide if they will enter the time machine again, or stay with their aged family and friends.

Students formed a circle. They told the others their decision and offered reasons for their choice.

Beyond the Drama

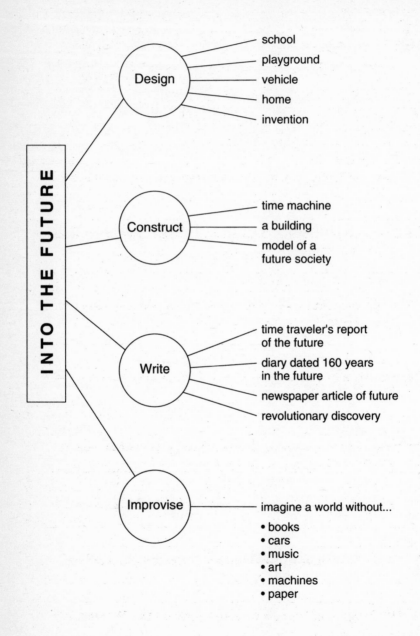

INTO THE FUTURE

Design
- school
- playground
- vehicle
- home
- invention

Construct
- time machine
- a building
- model of a future society

Write
- time traveler's report of the future
- diary dated 160 years in the future
- newspaper article of future
- revolutionary discovery

Improvise
- imagine a world without...
  - books
  - cars
  - music
  - art
  - machines
  - paper

Student Self-Assessment:
Focus on Improvisation Skills

Name: _____ Date: _____

1. Did you "believe" in imaginary situations?
   _____
   _____

2. What did you enjoy about improvising?
   _____
   _____

3. How did your ideas build and deepen the group's drama?
   _____
   _____

4. Do you prefer being involved in improvisation or watching others improvise?
   _____
   _____

5. What element might have improved the improvisations you took part in?
   _____
   _____

6. How is non-verbal improvisation different from improvised conversations?
   _____
   _____

7. What did you enjoy most about role playing characters?
   _____
   _____

8. How much "self" did you find in the roles you played?
   _____
   _____

9. What did you learn about drama from this dramatheme?
   _____
   _____

10. What did you learn about yourself from this dramatheme?
   _____
   _____

10/Multiculturalism

✻ "Because children come from varying backgrounds with different attitudes, values and circumstances, the responses they have to a text are all individual – and all legitimate. Each reader must paint his or her own story picture. Two readers may read the same book, but the stories they read will never completely match."

David Booth, *Classroom Voices* (1994, p. 137)

· · · · ·

Focus: Script

My blood is red. Your blood is red. Our blood is red. We are the same and different. By sliding into the skin of others, this dramatheme has students working together to gain an understanding of those who have opinions, values, cultures, and "skins" both like and unlike their own.

Learning Opportunities

- To develop skills of co-operation by playing games and working towards presenting a piece of work
- To examine the concept of racism and stereotypes by exploring a script
- To use script as a stimulus for role playing and improvisation
- To explore ways that text can be read aloud
- To use minimal scripts as a model for developing original scripts

Games: Focus on Co-operation

Co-operative Tag

In this game of tag, everyone is "It" at the same time that everyone is being chased. The object of the game is for a player to tag someone before being tagged. When tagged, the player freezes and stands with his or her legs spread apart. To be defrosted, the frozen player must have another person crawl through his or her legs. Confusion may result in who was tagged first – sorting out such problems develops co-operative skills.

VARIATIONS

- In Elbow Tag, "It" can tag someone only if she or he has not linked arms with another player. When tagged, the player becomes "It."
- In Amoebae Tag, "It" is an amoebae who tries to tag other players. If tagged, the player links arms with the amoebae and becomes part of "It." Other players can only be tagged by the free arm of players on either end of the growing amoebae. The object of the game is to tag all players.

Discussing Values

Students brainstorm as a class qualities they think are valuable in life. These might be qualities they admire in others, or qualities they think they possess, for example: honesty, intelligence, a sense of humor, curiosity, creativity, cheerfulness, optimism, perseverance, politeness, helpfulness, wisdom, charity, flexibility, and compassion.

Each student is given three slips of paper on which to record qualities she or he would like as a permanent part of their character. When finished, all slips of paper are put in a pile, and students choose three new slips. Students then barter with others in order to have the three qualities they most value. Through the course of the activity, students may change their mind on their original qualities. The bartering continues for approximately ten minutes. On a signal, students keep the qualities they have in hand, report them to the rest of the class, and determine their level of satisfaction. Finally, the class holds a survey to discover the most valued qualities and prioritizes those most essential to well-being.

Dot to Dot

This activity helps students to develop non-verbal skills. In order to complete the activity, students need adhesive dots in four colors. There should be equal numbers of dots in each color. Students sit in a circle with their eyes closed while a dot is randomly applied to their forehead. On a signal, they open their eyes and, without speaking, form groups of the same colored dots. This is a difficult activity because students do not know the color of the dot on their head and cannot speak through the activity.

EXTENSIONS

- Students form groups in which each member has a different colored dot.
- Colors can be distributed unevenly so that there will be smaller and larger groups.
- To make the groupings more complicated, two colors join together to make another group.

On the Line

This activity helps students to build an appreciation of the opinions of others. To begin, an imaginary line is drawn down the centre of the room. One end of the line represents the position of "strongly agree"; the other end, "strongly disagree." A statement on an issue is called out. Students move to a place on the line that expresses their opinion on the statement. The degree of support or opposition to the statement is evidenced by the students' position on the line. Students with no opinion on a statement stand at the centre of the line. All students should be encouraged to express their opinion through their position on the line, and not be swayed by the majority – they do not have to defend their point of view. From time to time, however, students may wish to express their feelings about a topic, or the class may wish to hold a spontaneous discussion on a topic of particular interest. Here are some suggested statements:

- It's important to study math.
- You should wear something because it's in style and not because you like it.
- Competition is good.
- You should never talk to strangers.

- School should be only four days a week. The length of the school day would be increased to make up for the missing day.
- Girls should be allowed to play on boys' sports teams.
- Honesty is the best policy.
- People should not be allowed to buy guns.

- Students share their opinions on a controversial topic through the use of a panel discussion or a debate. At the end of the discussion, they go back to the line to show their opinion.

Notes: Younger students can play this game by expressing their opinion on simple topics, for example, red is better than blue, crayons are better than paint, and dogs are friendlier than cats.

"The Line" is a useful strategy to use in a drama where students give their opinion about a character's behavior or a conflict that arises in the drama. They return to the line throughout a drama to see how their opinions have changed.

Dramatic Activities: Focus on Interpretion

Minimal Scripts

Students, with a partner, experiment with ways of saying the following lines aloud.

I'll see you again.
   Next week.
Perhaps.
   Very well.

I'm sorry.
   What?
I said I'm sorry.
   Sorry's just a word.

Do you like me?
   Yes.
Do you like me?
   Yes.
Do you like me?
   Why do you keep asking?

As the following lines are called out, partners practise saying the lines aloud. In each pair, one partner is assigned the role of "A"; the second, the role of "B."

- say the lines aloud
- reverse roles
- say the lines in a whisper
- say the lines as though talking on a telephone
- one person says the lines angrily; the other, calmly
- both partners say the lines angrily
- pause for a few seconds between lines
- sing the lines
- say the lines quickly
- do an activity while saying the lines
- shake hands
- make no eye contact
- sit back to back
- stare at each other
- shout across the room
- one partner shows no interest in the conversation
- say the lines in a sad voice
- read the lines while playing a clapping game

To change the dialogue, the following contexts for conducting the conversation can be suggested, or students choose an item. Items are printed on cards – partners pick up a card and develop an improvisation.

Roles	Activities	Settings
alien	baking a cake	in a restaurant
grandparent	fixing a bicycle	in a cave
child	writing a letter	on the seashore
soldier	eating an apple	on a train
nurse	reading a book	in an attic
principal	wallpapering	in a church
minister	working on a computer	in a graveyard
thief	getting dressed	in the library
dentist	building a tower	in the sandbox

- Students continue the conversations by adding to the dialogue.
- Students use the minimal scripts to end a conversation, rather than to begin a conversation.
- Students write a short script by adding lines of dialogue to the minimal script. Pairs exchange scripts and prepare them for each other.
- Instead of working in pairs, students work in groups of three or four. They note how the conversation changes when more than two people are involved.

One Liners

Students work with one liners to begin conversations and develop an improvisation between two or more characters. As students work with any of the following one liners, they invent the characters and the situation that inspires the conversation. Students experiment with characters, voice, and settings to influence the context for the conversations.

1. Are you all right?
2. This is the last time I'm going to warn you.
3. Come in.
4. I don't believe it!
5. Please accept my apologies.
6. Do you think you can keep a secret?
7. I don't know what you have against me.
8. What's your excuse this time?
9. Please leave me alone.
10. I don't think I can go today.
11. You're making a mountain out of a mole hole.
12. Where on earth did you put that thing?
13. Something should be done about it immediately.
14. Why can't you see anything from my point of view?
15. I'd rather not say.
16. How much did you say?
17. Shhh!
18. Are you ready yet?

Students experiment with the one liners by using these strategies:

- With a partner, choose a one liner and discuss who might be speaking, where they might be, and why they might be having the conversation. The one liner is then used to begin a conversation.
- Instead of beginning a conversation with the one liner, prepare an improvisation in which the one liner is the last line of the conversation.
- One partner chooses a one liner. After she or he has said the line, the partner continues it. Partners accept each other's responses even if they are thinking of different situations. The object is to continue the conversation as long as possible.
- Experiment with ways of saying lines, for example, by raising or lowering voices, by stressing certain words, by using gestures, by changing eye contact, and by sitting or standing in a certain position.
- Perform an activity while having a conversation (e.g., fixing a bicycle).
- Work in groups of four or five. One person introduces a line to the group; each member finds a way to fit it into the conversation.

Extended Improvisation: Using a Script – "Skin"

This section centres on the play "Skin" by Dennis Foon. Each scene in the play deals with a different aspect of racism or prejudice. Its effectiveness in promoting dialogue on these issues has been proved in countless classrooms, and its content and style make it an effective tool to use in drama exploration. The following outline details the work a class of grade seven/eight students completed around the script.

Session One

Whole-Class Interpretation
To begin, students read the opening twenty-six lines aloud as a whole class. Each student, in a clockwise direction, read aloud

one of the lines. The activity was repeated by having students read the lines in a counter-clockwise direction. In this way, each student had the chance to read aloud two lines. Reading aloud in a variety of ways helped the students to understand that a line of dialogue can mean different things depending on the way it is read aloud. Meaning can be altered by:

- stressing or emphasizing certain words (emphasis),
- raising or lowering the voice (pitch),
- reading lines slowly or quickly (pace).

Students explored this minimal script by:

- reading the script aloud as quickly as possible,
- pausing between the reading of each line,
- reading lines aloud from a whisper to a shout and vice versa,
- emphasizing one word in the line,
- reading the line in a manner that was different than the way the last line was read,
- adding a gesture as the line was read aloud,
- using gesture or movement only,
- reading cumulatively, that is, one person began reading from the first line – a few seconds later, the next person began reading from the first line and so on until each person had read the script aloud,
- reading the lines as if they were alien creatures (or elves, robots, clowns),
- rearranging the order in which the lines were read.

After exploring the introductory script to "Skin," some students in the class chose to model the lines to create their own poem that could be used to introduce this play. This example was written by one grade seven student:

I am five feet two inches tall.
I weigh 130 pounds.
I have one nose.
One neck.
One face.
One brain.
One heart.
Two eyes.
Two hands.
Ten fingers.

Ten toes.
I can move.
I can sit.
I can think.
I can dream.
My heart is red.
My heart is red.
My heart is red.
My heart is red.
I smile.
I cry.
I feel.
I breathe.
I hope.
I hope.
I hope.
I hope.

Liza T.

Small-Group Interpretation

To further practise techniques of interpretation, the class was divided into small groups of four or five members. Each group experimented with ways of dividing the lines among the group. Some lines were read as solo, some in pairs, and some as a whole group. Students were encouraged to practise emphasis, pitch, and pace.

I asked the students to consider actions and gestures that would complement or accentuate the meaning behind the words. As a group, they made decisions about:

• standing or sitting,
• beginning or ending with stillness,
• adding gestures as lines were read.

Groups shared their rehearsed interpretations of these lines with one another.

Note: As a further problem-solving activity, two groups can work together to interpret this script. Groups can combine ideas for their original presentations to work on a new interpretation of this scene.

Session Two

Improvisation

The class discussed the prologue in order to better understand the message the playwright was conveying through the opening lines. I asked the students several questions, including: what message was he trying to convey in these lines, why would he use short lines and repeat some of these lines, do some or all of the lines seem to apply to specific characters, and what event might have precipitated the speaking of these lines.

In pairs or groups of three, students prepared an improvised scene that attempted to explain why someone might give this monologue, including:

• who might be saying these lines,
• how the person was feeling,
• where the lines might have been said,
• who would have listened to these lines.

Note: To increase their understanding of circumstances, students should be helped to understand the circumstances that would make someone say this monologue. Each group can prepare an improvisation that could serve as a prologue to the scripted scene. In context of the theme of "Skin," the improvisation will likely focus on an incident that depicts racism, prejudice, rejection, teasing, or antagonism.

Session Three

Hot Seating

In hot seating, students assume the role of a character from a novel, poem, play, or story. When they take the hot seat, they are interviewed by classmates or group members who want to discover more about the character – how she or he feels about events, people, and places. Assuming the hot seat allows students to solidify their perceptions of a character.

In this dramatheme, hot seating was a useful strategy to have students speculate about the causes of prejudice and racism in some young people. In order to discover more about the attitudes and motivations of those who have caused trouble, several students volunteered to takes on roles portrayed in previous improvisations and be hot-seated by the rest of the group about their attitudes to school, community, family, and so on.

Session Four

Preparing Scripts

Students worked in small groups to prepare an original script, that is, a short piece of dialogue that did not include notes on speakers and what prompted them to speak as they did. The intent of a minimal script is to make the dialogue and the situation as open-ended as possible. For this activity, the students prepared scenes that occured before and after "Skin" was written. Groups exchanged their finished scripts and rehearsed presentations of the scenes. An alternative would have been to have two groups work together to share their presentations. This increases co-operation as a number of students have to make decisions regarding adding or deleting lines from the script. The minimal scripts were then assembled to make a co-operative script called "Skin."

Beyond the Drama

Working with the Script

Students work with other scenes that appear in "Skin." Each scene depicts an aspect of racism or prejudice. Students practise ways of interpreting the scene by reading it aloud, and then create an improvisation that demonstrates the problem that the character(s) encounter. In groups, students prepare a presentation of the play. Given its open-endedness, several students can play the same character.

> A monologue is a short speech that a character gives to an audience. The character can use the monologue as a vehicle to express his or her feelings and thoughts on a subject or event, or to tell a story or anecdote.

Using a character that they have role played during an improvisation, students prepare a monologue that conveys their characters' feelings about prejudice. When finished, they read their monologues aloud to an audience (whole class or small groups). A decision should be made about the audience for this monologue (who would the person be speaking to and why). After reading the monologue, students answer questions in role.

First-Person Poem

Students prepare a list poem using the opening scene of "Skin" as a model. Writing their poems in first-person voice, students can write about:

- themselves,
- a character they have role played in the drama,
- a historical figure,
- a character from a novel,
- a person featured in the news,
- a character who appears in the play.

Collage

Using magazine or newspaper photos, students create a multicultural collage or mural that might be entitled "Skin." Students use words or phrases found in headlines or captions that could be suitable for use in their collage.

Images of "Skin"

Students consider an image they think best suits the monologue presented in the opening scene. Students prepare images:

- as a sculpture that would convey this character's feelings, or
- as a cover design that might be used for a published version of the play "Skin."

Assessment: Focus on Interpretation

Name: _____ Date: _____

Does the student:	Always	Sometimes	Never
1. Investigate many possibilities of using voice to read the text aloud?	☐	☐	☐
2. Experiment with gesture?	☐	☐	☐
3. Explore various ways of moving, standing, or sitting?	☐	☐	☐
4. Work effectively in role to interpret script?	☐	☐	☐
5. Seem able to improvise dialogue?	☐	☐	☐
6. Accept advice?	☐	☐	☐
7. Offer suggestions for shaping and presenting script?	☐	☐	☐
8. Work with a number of partners?	☐	☐	☐
9. Seem to understand the author's intent?	☐	☐	☐
10. Seem engaged with the activity?	☐	☐	☐

Comments:

_____

_____

_____

_____

_____

_____

_____

_____

Appendix

Drama Reflections

Name: _____ Date: _____

1. Which game(s) did you enjoy playing the most?
_____

2. Which drama activity/activities appealed to you the most?
_____

3. Which do you prefer – watching others role play a character or taking part in role play?
_____

4. What does role playing teach you?
_____

5. How does drama help you build your imagination?
_____

6. How does drama help you to co-operate?
_____

7. What advice would you give to someone who wants to take a drama course?
_____

8. What did you learn about drama by participating in drama activities?
_____

9. What did you learn about yourself by participating in drama activities?
_____

10. What do you like most about drama?
_____

11. What do you like least about drama?
_____

12. I would improve ...
_____
_____

Drama Profile

Name: _____ Date: _____

For each question, place a check mark in the column that you think best describes your feelings about working in drama.

	Agree	Neither Agree nor Disagree	Disagree
1. I enjoy drama	_____	_____	_____
2. I enjoy playing games	_____	_____	_____
3. I enjoy working with different partners	_____	_____	_____
4. I enjoy working in small groups	_____	_____	_____
5. I enjoy working in whole-class activities	_____	_____	_____
6. I felt comfortable working in role	_____	_____	_____
7. Drama gives me the chance to share my ideas	_____	_____	_____
8. Drama helps me to solve problems	_____	_____	_____
9. Drama gives me the opportunity to deal with emotions	_____	_____	_____
10. Drama is for everybody	_____	_____	_____

Circle three qualities that best describe your success as a drama student.

- trustworthy
- co-operative
- confident
- imaginative
- curious
- playful
- conscientious
- leader
- good listener
- risk taker

Put a check mark beside three qualities that you wish you had.

What does drama mean to you ?

_____

_____

_____

Drama Observation Guide

Name: _____ Date: _____

Scale:

1	2	3	4	5
needs improvement (1)			to a great	extent (5)

Participation: Involvement and Social Development

Investigates possibilities, contributes ideas   1 2 3 4 5

Works well alone, in pairs, in small groups,
and as part of whole class   1 2 3 4 5

Co-operates and supports the contributions
of others   1 2 3 4 5

Complies with instructions and is committed
to the work   1 2 3 4 5

Appears to enjoy drama   1 2 3 4 5

Comments:

_____

_____

Communication: Language and Physical Development

Communicates ideas orally   1 2 3 4 5

Raises questions   1 2 3 4 5

Uses drama to write effectively   1 2 3 4 5

Demonstrates skill in reading aloud   1 2 3 4 5

Interprets ideas through the body
(e.g., tableau, mime)   1 2 3 4 5

Enjoys games and movement activities   1 2 3 4 5

Comments:

_____

Imagination: Dramatic and Aesthetic Awareness

Appears to be imaginative, creative   1 2 3 4 5

Willing to reveal thoughts and feelings   1 2 3 4 5

Understands and works effectively in role   1 2 3 4 5

Uses effectively the forms of drama
(e.g., tableau, mime, storytelling)   1 2 3 4 5

Able to reflect on the meaning of drama   1 2 3 4 5

Comments:

_____

Recommended Books

Chapter One: Humor

Becker, L. & M. Stratton. 1988. *Little Miss Muffet*. Freemont, CA: Worlds of Wonder.

Booth, D. 1993. *Doctor Knickerbocker and Other Rhymes*. Toronto, ON: Kids Can Press; New York, NY: Ticknor and Field Books for Young Readers.

Dunn, S. 1990. *Crackers and Crumbs: Chants for Whole Language*. Markham, ON: Pembroke Publishers; Portsmouth, NH: Heinemann.

Foreman, M. 1991. *Michael Foreman's Mother Goose*. San Diego, CA: Harcourt Brace & Company.

Graham, C. 1994. *Mother Goose Jazz Chants*. New York, NY: Oxford University Press.

Lottridge, C. 1994. *Mother Goose: A Canadian Sampler*. Toronto, ON: Groundwood Books.

Opie, I. & P. 1992. *I Saw Esau*. Cambridge, MA: Candlewick Press.

Schwartz, A. 1992. *And The Green Grass Grew All Around: Folk Poetry for Everyone*. New York, NY: HarperCollins Children's Books.

Chapter Two: Mystery

De Regniers, B. et al. 1988. *Sing a Song of Popcorn: Every Child's Book of Poems*. New York, NY: Scholastic, Inc.

Greenfield, E. 1991. *Night on Neighborhood Street*. New York, NY: Dial Books for Young Readers.

Huck, C. 1993. *Secret Places*. New York, NY: Greenwillow Books.

o'huigan, s. 1991. *Ghost Horse of the Mounties*. Windsor, ON: Black Moss Press; Boston, MA: David R. Godine Publishers, Inc.

Patten, B. 1991. *The Puffin Book of Twentieth Century Verse*. London, U.K.: Puffin.

Rosen, M.J. 1994. *The Greatest Table: A Banquet to Fight Against Hunger.* San Diego, CA: Harcourt Brace & Company.

Wood, N. 1993. *Spirit Walker: Poems.* New York, NY: Delacorte Press.

Chapter Three: Fantasy

Barton, B. 1990. *The Reindeer Herder and the Moon.* London, U.K.: BBC Educational Publishers.

Bruchac, J. & J. London. 1992. *Thirteen Moons on Turtle's Back: A Native American Year of Moons.* New York, NY: The Putnam Publishing Group.

Ehlert, L. 1992. *Moon Rope: A Peruvian Folktale/Un Lazo a la Luna: Una Leyenda Peruana.* San Diego, CA: Harcourt Brace & Company.

Morgan, N. 1991. *Louis and the Night Sky.* New York, NY: Oxford University Press.

Willard, N. 1983. *The Nightgown of the Sullen Moon.* San Diego, CA: Harcourt Brace & Company.

Wynne-Jones, T. 1988. *Architect of the Moon.* Toronto, ON: Groundwood Books.

Chapter Four: Animals

Bierhorst, J. 1987. *Doctor Coyote: A Native American Aesop's Fables.* New York, NY: Macmillan Children's Book Group.

Cohen, M. 1989. *The Puffin Book of Fabulous Fables.* London, U.K.: Puffin Books.

Lobel, A. 1980. *Fables.* New York, NY: HarperCollins Children's Books.

Lottridge, C. 1994. *Ten Small Tales.* Toronto, ON: Douglas & McIntyre; New York, NY: Macmillan Children's Book Group.

Rosen, M.J. 1994. *South and North, East and West: The Oxfam Book of Children's Stories.* Cambridge, MA: Candlewick Press.

Salter, S. (illus.). 1992. *Aesop's Fables.* San Diego, CA: Harcourt Brace & Company.

Testa, F. (illus.). 1989. *Aesop's Fables.* Hauppauge, NY: Barron's Educational Series Inc.

Thornhill, J. 1993. *Crow and Fox and Other Animal Legends.* Toronto, ON: Greey de Pencier.

Chapter Five: Relationships

Andrews, J. 1991. *The Auction*. Toronto, ON: Groundwood Books; New York, NY: Macmillan Children's Book Group.

Essley, R. 1994. *Reunion*. New York, NY: Simon & Schuster, Inc.

Fox, M. 1989. *Night Noises*. San Diego, CA: Harcourt Brace & Company.

Fox, M. 1985. *Wilfrid Gordon McDonald Partridge*. Brooklyn, NY: Kane/Miller Book Publishers.

MacLachlan, P. 1991. *Journey*. New York, NY: Delacorte Press.

Oberman, S. 1994. *The Always Prayer Shawl*. Honesdale, PA: Boyds Mill Press.

Waddell, M. 1990. *Grandma's Bill*. New York, NY: Orchard Books.

Yardley, J. 1991. *The Red Ball*. San Diego, CA: Harcourt Brace & Company.

Chapter Six: Folklore

Emberley, M. 1990. *Ruby*. New York, NY: Little Brown & Company.

Graham, C. 1988. *Jazz Chant Fairy Tales*. New York, NY: Oxford University Press.

Little, J. & M. de Vries. 1991. *Once Upon A Golden Apple*. New York, NY: Viking Children's Books.

Marshall, J. 1990. *Little Red Riding Hood*. Boston, MA: Houghton Mifflin Co.

Pearlman, J. 1994. *The Emperor Penguin's New Clothes*. Toronto, ON: Kids Can Press.

Scieszka, J. 1989. *The True Story of the Three Little Pigs*. New York, NY: Viking Children's Books.

Young, E. 1989. *Lon Po Po: A Red Riding Hood Story from China*. New York, NY: The Putnam Publishing Group.

Wilson, D.H. 1990. "Little Red Riding Hood: The Wolf's Story" from *There's a Wolf in My Pudding*. London, U.K.: J.M. Dent & Sons.

Chapter Seven: Community

Blos, J. 1987. *Old Henry*. New York, NY: Morrow Junior Books.

Brown, R. 1990. *The House that Jack Built*. Toronto, ON: Stoddart.

Gantschev, I. 1985. *Two Islands*. Boston, MA: Picture Book Studio Ltd.

Greenfield, E. 1991. *Night on Neighborhood Street*. New York, NY: Dial Books for Young Readers.

Hartman, G. 1991. *As The Crow Flies: A First Book of Maps*. New York, NY: Macmillan Children's Book Group.

Lionni, L. 1989. *Tillie and the Wall*. New York, NY: Alfred A. Knopf Books for Young Readers.

Parry Heide, F. & J. Gilliland. 1992. *Sami and the Time of Troubles*. Boston, MA: Houghton Mifflin Co.

Provensen, A. & M. 1987. *Shaker Lane*. New York, NY: Viking Children's Books.

Snape, J. & C. 1989. *Giant*. London, U.K.: Walker Books Ltd.

Chapter Eight: The Past

Hamilton, V. 1992. *Many Thousand Gone: African-Americans from Slavery to Freedom*. New York, NY: Alfred A. Knopf Books for Young Readers.

Krull, K. 1992. *Gonna Sing My Head Off: American Folk Songs for Children*. New York, NY: Alfred A. Knopf Books for Young Readers.

Paulsen, G. 1993. *Nightjohn*. New York, NY: Delacorte Press.

Ringgold, F. 1992. *Aunt Harriet's Underground Railroad in the Sky*. New York, NY: Crown Books for Young Readers.

Smucker, B. 1977. *Underground to Canada*. Concord, ON: Irwin Publishing.

Chapter Nine: The Future

Babbitt, N. 1985. *Tuck Everlasting*. New York, NY: Farrar, Straus & Giroux.

Fleischman, P. 1991. *Time Train*. New York, NY: HarperCollins Children's Books.

Sadler, M. 1989. *Alistair's Time Machine*. London, U.K.: Hamish Hamilton; New York, NY: Simon & Schuster, Inc.

Scieszka, H. 1995. *2095*. New York, NY: Viking Children's Books.

Van Allsburg, C. 1991. *The Wretched Stone*. Boston, MA: Houghton Mifflin Co.

Wiesner, D. 1993. *June 29, 1993*. Boston, MA: Houghton Mifflin Co.

Chapter Ten: Multiculturalism

Hubley, F. & J. 1973. *The Hat*. San Diego, CA: Harcourt Brace & Company.

Littlejohn, G. 1993. *This Land Is My Land*. Emeryville, CA: Children's Book Press.

McGugan, J. 1994. *Josepha*. Red Deer, AB: Red Deer College Press; San Francisco, CA: Chronicle Books.

Polacco, P. 1992. *Chicken Sunday*. New York, NY: The Putnam Publishing Group.

Raschka, C. 1993. *Yo! Yes?* New York, NY: Orchard Books.

Spinelli, J. 1990. *Maniac McGee*. Boston, MA: Little Brown & Company.

Professional Reading

Bob Barton
Tell Me Another
Pembroke Publishers Limited: Markham, Ontario
Heinemann: Portsmouth, New Hampshire, 1986

Storyteller Bob Barton explores the world of using story in chapters that include information on selecting a story, learning a story, reading a story, and using storytelling in the classroom.

David Booth
Classroom Voices: Language-Based Learning in the Elementary School
Harcourt Brace & Company, Canada: Toronto, Ontario, 1994

This textbook presents current information about language learning, and describes authentic practical experiences from teachers at one Canadian school. In particular, Chapter 4 highlights the role of drama by outlining such topics as dramatic play, planning for drama, choral dramatization, reflecting and presenting, and performing.

David Booth
Story Drama: Reading, Writing and Roleplaying across the Curriculum
Pembroke Publishers: Markham, Ontario, 1994

David Booth argues that role play is a natural way in which young people can explore the world. This book, written as a memoir of the author's extensive work with children, provides classroom models and frameworks for creating an enriching interactive environment.

David Booth and Bob Barton
Stories in the Classroom: Storytelling, Reading & Roleplaying with Children
Pembroke Publishers: Markham, Ontario;
Heinemann: Portsmouth, New Hampshire, 1990

The authors describe a comprehensive overview of choosing and using stories in the classroom.

Richard Courtney
Play, Drama and Thought (Revised)
Simon & Pierre: Toronto, Ontario, 1991

Courtney, arguing that human drama is a process that under-lies all education, shares his views from philosophical, psychological, sociological, and anthropological perspectives.

Susan Engels
The Stories Children Tell: Making Sense of the Narratives of Childhood
W.H. Freeman and Company: New York, New York, 1995

Taking the view that narrative is a prime way of making meaning, the author shows how children use storytelling to construct imaginary realms and to form their understandings of self and world.

Mem Fox
Teaching Drama to Young Children
Heinemann: Portsmouth, New Hampshire, 1987

A resource for teachers of children ages five to eight who would like to teach drama but are not sure of how to begin.

Jeanne Gibbs
Tribes: A New Way of Learning Together
Center Source Publications: Santa Rosa, California, 1978 (1994)

This guide describes a process for social development and co-operative learning groups. One hundred and twenty activities, a resource list, and information on training are provided.

Dorothy Heathcote and Gavin Bolton
Drama for Learning: Dorothy Heathcote's Mantle of the Expert Approach to Education
Heinemann: Portsmouth, New Hampshire, 1995

Using drama as an impetus for productive learning across the curriculum, Dorothy Heathcote's mantle of the expert approach uses a problem or task for teachers and students, in role, to explore the knowledge they already have while making new discoveries along the way.

Nancy King
Storymaking and Drama: An Approach to Teaching Language at the Secondary and Postsecondary Level
Heinemann: Portsmouth, New Hampshire, 1993

King demonstrates how storymaking and drama are powerful ways to engage students as they experience novels, play, poetry, and autobiography.

Alan Maley and Alan Duff
Drama Techniques in Language Learning: A Resource Book of Communication Activities for Language Teachers
Cambridge University Press: New York, New York, 1983

This book details a large selection of techniques for use at all levels that focus learning on communication tasks and activities.

Lucy McCormick Calkins and Shelley Harwayne
Living Between the Lines
Heinemann: Portsmouth, New Hampshire, 1991

Chapter Twelve, "Memoirs: Reading and Writing the Stories of Our Lives" has particular relevance to material presented in this book.

John McLeod
Drama Is Real Pretending
Ministry of Education (Schools Division): Victoria, Australia, 1988

This book offers a comprehensive approach to teaching drama and developing drama curriculum. Specific chapters draw attention to designing lessons, developing a whole program, the teacher's role, and assessing and evaluating the learning.

Norah Morgan and Julianna Saxton
Asking Better Questions
Pembroke Publishers: Markham, Ontario, 1994

The authors provide a thorough examination of teacher and student questioning to promote language and cognitive growth.

Jonothan Neelands
Learning through Imagined Experience
Hodder & Stoughton: London, England, 1992

Neelands demonstrates how drama, incorporated into topic work, is indispensable for providing opportunities for "real talk" to help children make sense of context and language use.

Jonothan Neelands, edited by Tony Goode
Structuring Drama Work: A Handbook of Available Forms in Theatre & Drama
Cambridge University Press: New York, New York, 1990

Neelands offers a complete range of theatrical conventions that serve to initiate, focus, and develop dramatic activity.

Cecily O'Neill and Allan Lambert
Drama Structures: A Practical Handbook for Teachers
Hutchinson: London, England, 1982

Fifteen lesson themes involve students in a wide range of drama and learning activities.

Vivian Gussin Paley
You Can't Say You Can't Play
Harvard University Press: Cambridge, Massachusetts, 1993

The author describes authentic experiences with her kindergarten children when she puts a single rule in place to promote cooperation and collaboration.

Anna Sher and Charles Verral
100 + Drama Ideas
Heinemann Educational Books: Oxford, England

This collection is an "ideas" resource full of dramatic and improvisation strategies that have been used with both young people and adults.

Carole Tarlington and Wendy Michaels
Building Plays: Simple Playbuilding Techniques at Work
Pembroke Publishers: Markham, Ontario;
Heinemann: Portsmouth, New Hampshire, 1995

Included in this practical introduction to playbuilding are outlines for building a play in a day, using Shakespeare as a source for playbuilding, and the highly successful "Immigrant Stories."

Index